Mastering Load Testing with JMeter and Locust

Simulating User Traffic, Identifying Performance Bottlenecks, and Optimizing Response Times for Scalable Web and API Services

Greyson Chesterfield

COPYRIGHT

Chapter 1: Introduction to Load Testing

Definition of Load Testing

Load testing is a type of performance testing that simulates the conditions of actual user traffic to assess how a system behaves under varying levels of load. This includes measuring system performance metrics such as response times, throughput, and resource utilization under different loads. Load testing is essential for understanding the system's capacity to handle concurrent users and transactions without degradation of performance. It provides valuable insights into how the system will perform in a production environment, allowing developers and testers to identify potential issues before deployment.

Load testing can be performed on various types of applications, including web applications, APIs, and microservices. The primary goal is to ensure that the system can handle anticipated peak loads and identify any performance bottlenecks that may hinder its operation. By simulating real-world usage scenarios, load testing helps to ensure that applications can scale effectively and maintain a high-quality user experience, even under heavy loads.

Importance of Load Testing in Software Development

In today's digital landscape, applications are expected to deliver seamless performance regardless of user volume. The increasing reliance on web-based services necessitates robust load testing practices to avoid performance-related issues that can lead to poor user experience, loss of revenue, and damage to brand reputation. Here are some reasons why load testing is crucial in software development:

Ensuring Reliability and Stability: Load testing helps ensure that applications can withstand high levels of traffic and continue to function reliably. By identifying weak points in the system, developers can address issues before they impact users.

Validating Scalability: As businesses grow, their applications must be able to scale efficiently to accommodate increasing numbers of users. Load testing validates that the architecture can handle growth and identifies limits to scalability.

Preventing Downtime: Performance issues can lead to system failures and downtime, which can be costly for businesses. Load testing helps detect potential failure points and allows for corrective measures to be implemented before production deployment.

Improving User Experience: Slow response times and application crashes can frustrate users. Load testing helps ensure that applications respond quickly and consistently, leading to higher user satisfaction and retention.

Cost Efficiency: Identifying and fixing performance issues in the development stage is more cost-effective than addressing them after deployment. Load testing helps to minimize the likelihood of costly fixes and downtime.

Supporting Continuous Integration/Continuous Deployment (CI/CD): In modern development practices, where CI/CD is a standard approach, load testing becomes vital. Automated load tests can be integrated into the CI/CD pipeline to ensure that performance is continually monitored and validated as new code is deployed.

Overview of Common Tools and Methodologies

Various tools and methodologies are available for conducting load testing, each with its strengths and suitable use cases. Choosing the right tool depends on the specific requirements of the application, the technology stack, and the testing objectives.

Common Load Testing Tools:

Apache JMeter: A popular open-source tool designed for load testing and performance measurement of both web applications and APIs. JMeter allows testers to create complex test scenarios and analyze results through comprehensive reports and graphs.

Locust: An open-source load testing tool that allows users to write test scenarios in Python. Locust is particularly well-suited for testing web applications and APIs with a focus on ease of use and scalability.

LoadRunner: A commercial performance testing tool that supports a wide range of protocols and technologies. LoadRunner is widely used in enterprise environments and offers advanced features for monitoring and analysis.

Gatling: An open-source load testing tool that focuses on ease of use and high performance. Gatling allows users to write tests in Scala and provides detailed reports on performance metrics.

k6: A modern load testing tool that enables users to write test scripts in JavaScript. k6 is designed for developer-focused testing and is particularly well-suited for testing APIs.

Common Methodologies:

Scenario-Based Testing: This approach involves simulating specific user scenarios, such as browsing a website or submitting a form. Scenarios can be defined based on expected user behavior to provide realistic testing conditions.

Stress Testing: Stress testing evaluates how a system behaves under extreme conditions, often beyond its maximum capacity. The goal is to identify failure points and assess system recovery.

Endurance Testing: Endurance testing, also known as soak testing, evaluates system performance over an extended period under a specified load. This method helps identify memory leaks and performance degradation over time.

Spike Testing: This method assesses the system's ability to handle sudden spikes in user traffic. By rapidly increasing the load, testers can determine how well the system can adapt to sudden changes.

Capacity Testing: Capacity testing aims to determine the maximum number of concurrent users the system can handle while maintaining acceptable performance levels. This information is crucial for capacity planning and resource allocation.

Key Objectives of Load Testing

The primary objectives of load testing can be summarized as follows:

Determine System Behavior Under Load: Load testing provides insights into how the system responds to increasing user loads, helping to identify performance bottlenecks and areas for improvement.

Validate Performance Criteria: By defining specific performance criteria—such as acceptable response times and throughput—load testing ensures that the system meets its performance goals.

Identify Performance Bottlenecks: Load testing helps pinpoint areas where performance may degrade, such as slow database queries, insufficient server resources, or network latency.

Assess Scalability: Load testing evaluates the system's ability to scale horizontally or vertically to handle increased user traffic without sacrificing performance.

Ensure Resource Utilization: Effective load testing assesses how well the system utilizes its resources, including CPU, memory, and network bandwidth, to ensure efficient operation.

Facilitate Continuous Improvement: Load testing is an iterative process that helps teams continually improve application performance by providing feedback on changes made during development.

In summary, load testing is a critical component of modern software development practices. It ensures that applications are reliable, scalable, and capable of delivering a high-quality user experience under varying load conditions. By leveraging the right tools and methodologies, teams can effectively simulate user traffic, identify performance bottlenecks, and optimize response times, ultimately contributing to the success of their web and API services.

Chapter 2: Understanding Performance Testing

Types of Performance Testing: Load Testing, Stress Testing, Endurance Testing, Spike Testing

Performance testing is an umbrella term that encompasses various testing types designed to assess the responsiveness, speed, scalability, and stability of a software application under a particular workload. Understanding the different types of performance testing is essential for selecting the right approach for your specific application and ensuring that it meets user expectations.

Load Testing: Load testing is designed to evaluate how a system performs under a specific expected load, which is defined as the number of concurrent users or transactions. The primary goal is to identify how the system behaves when subjected to realistic workloads and to measure key performance metrics such as response time, throughput, and resource utilization. Load testing helps determine the system's capacity limits and ensures that it can handle expected traffic levels without degrading performance.

Stress Testing: Stress testing takes load testing a step further by pushing the system beyond its defined capacity limits. The goal is to determine how the application behaves under extreme conditions, such as a sudden spike in traffic or a significant increase in data processing demands. Stress testing identifies the system's breaking point, allowing teams to understand how it behaves when it is overwhelmed. This testing type is essential for ensuring that the system can recover gracefully from overload conditions and for identifying potential failure points.

Endurance Testing: Also known as soak testing, endurance testing evaluates how the system performs under a sustained load over an extended period. The goal is to identify issues that may arise during prolonged use, such as memory leaks, resource exhaustion, or degradation of performance. Endurance testing is crucial for applications expected to operate continuously, such as web services and online platforms, as it helps ensure long-term stability and reliability.

Spike Testing: Spike testing involves subjecting the system to sudden and extreme increases in load, followed by a rapid decrease back to normal levels. This testing type helps evaluate how well the application can handle unexpected traffic spikes, such as those caused by marketing campaigns or viral content. By assessing how the system responds to abrupt changes in load, teams can identify potential weaknesses and areas for improvement in scalability and performance.

Understanding these types of performance testing is essential for creating effective testing strategies that align with the specific needs of the application and its users.

Differences Between Functional and Performance Testing

While functional testing and performance testing are both critical components of the software testing lifecycle, they serve different purposes and focus on different aspects of the application. Recognizing the differences between these two testing types is essential for ensuring comprehensive quality assurance.

Focus: Functional testing focuses on verifying that the application behaves as expected based on its functional requirements. This includes testing individual features and functionalities to ensure they work correctly according to specified criteria. In contrast, performance testing is concerned with how well the application performs under varying workloads and conditions. It measures metrics such as response times, throughput, and resource utilization, focusing on system behavior rather than specific functionalities.

Objectives: The primary objective of functional testing is to ensure that the application meets user requirements and performs the intended tasks correctly. Functional tests verify the correctness of features and ensure that all parts of the application work together seamlessly. On the other hand, performance testing aims to assess the application's scalability, reliability, and speed. It helps identify performance bottlenecks, evaluate system capacity, and ensure that the application can handle expected user loads without degradation.

Approach: Functional testing typically employs a variety of testing techniques, including manual testing, automated testing, and user acceptance testing (UAT). Test cases are often derived from functional specifications and user stories, focusing on specific features and user interactions.

Performance testing, however, relies on simulated user loads to evaluate system performance. Load testing tools, such as JMeter and Locust, are commonly used to automate performance tests and generate load conditions.

Timing: Functional testing is generally performed throughout the software development lifecycle, including during development, testing, and pre-release phases. It ensures that features are functioning correctly before the application is deployed. In contrast, performance testing is often conducted after functional testing, typically in staging or pre-production environments. This allows teams to focus on system performance and scalability once the application's features have been validated.

Understanding these differences is crucial for developing a comprehensive testing strategy that addresses both functional and performance aspects of the application. By integrating both types of testing, teams can ensure a high-quality product that meets user expectations and performs reliably under varying loads.

Key Metrics in Performance Testing: Response Time, Throughput, Error Rates

Measuring the performance of an application during load testing requires specific metrics to assess its responsiveness, capacity, and reliability. Understanding these metrics is essential for identifying performance issues and optimizing the system. The following key metrics are commonly used in performance testing:

Response Time: Response time is the total time it takes for the system to respond to a user's request. This metric is critical because it directly affects user experience; longer response times can lead to user frustration and abandonment of the application. Response time can be further broken down into various components, including:

Latency: The time taken for a request to travel from the client to the server.

Processing Time: The time taken by the server to process the request and generate a response.

Network Time: The time taken for the response to travel back to the client.

Performance testing typically measures average response time, but it's also essential to consider percentiles (e.g., 90th and 95th percentiles) to understand the distribution of response times under load.

Throughput: Throughput measures the number of requests that the system can handle in a given period, typically expressed as requests per second (RPS) or transactions per second (TPS). Throughput is a crucial metric for evaluating system capacity and scalability. A higher throughput indicates that the application can handle more user traffic effectively. During load testing, it's important to analyze how throughput varies with different loads, as this can reveal capacity limits and performance bottlenecks.

Error Rates: Error rates indicate the percentage of requests that result in errors during testing. This metric is essential for assessing the reliability of the application under load. Error rates can help identify issues such as server failures, database connection problems, or application bugs. Monitoring error rates during load testing provides insights into system stability and helps ensure that the application meets quality standards. High error rates may indicate performance bottlenecks or misconfigurations that need to be addressed before deployment.

In addition to these core metrics, other performance indicators may include resource utilization (CPU, memory, and disk usage), network latency, and the number of concurrent users. By analyzing these metrics during performance testing, teams can gain a comprehensive understanding of the application's behavior under load and identify areas for improvement.

Importance of Defining Performance Criteria

Defining performance criteria is a critical step in the load testing process. Performance criteria outline the expected performance levels that the application must meet to satisfy user requirements and business objectives. The following points highlight the importance of establishing clear performance criteria:

Setting Expectations: Performance criteria help establish clear expectations for system performance, providing stakeholders with benchmarks against which performance can be measured. By defining specific metrics such as response times, throughput, and error rates, teams can ensure that everyone has a shared understanding of what constitutes acceptable performance.

Guiding Testing Efforts: Clear performance criteria guide the design and execution of load tests. They help teams focus on the most relevant metrics and scenarios during testing, ensuring that efforts are aligned with business objectives. Without defined criteria, testing efforts may be unfocused and fail to provide meaningful insights.

Facilitating Decision-Making: Performance criteria enable informed decision-making by providing a framework for evaluating test results. By comparing actual performance against defined criteria, teams can determine whether the application meets quality standards and whether it is ready for deployment. This data-driven approach helps identify performance bottlenecks that require attention and improvement.

Supporting Continuous Improvement: Performance criteria serve as a baseline for measuring improvements over time. By regularly assessing performance against established benchmarks, teams can identify trends and make data-driven decisions to enhance application performance. Continuous improvement is essential in today's fast-paced software development environment, where user expectations evolve rapidly.

Mitigating Risks: Clearly defined performance criteria help mitigate risks associated with deploying applications that may not meet user demands. By establishing performance expectations early in the development process, teams can identify and address potential performance issues before they impact users. This proactive approach helps reduce the likelihood of costly fixes and downtime after deployment.

In summary, understanding the various types of performance testing, recognizing the differences between functional and performance testing, and monitoring key performance metrics are crucial components of ensuring application quality. By defining clear performance criteria, teams can set expectations, guide testing efforts, and make informed decisions that contribute to the overall success of the software. These foundational concepts in performance testing pave the way for effective load testing practices, ensuring that applications are reliable, scalable, and capable of delivering an exceptional user experience.

Chapter 3: Introduction to JMeter and Locust

Overview of JMeter

Apache JMeter is a widely-used open-source tool designed for load testing and performance measurement of various types of applications, including web applications, APIs, and databases. Originally developed for testing web applications, JMeter has evolved into a versatile tool that supports a wide range of protocols, making it a popular choice for performance testing in diverse environments.

JMeter operates on a client-server architecture, allowing users to simulate multiple virtual users and generate load on the system being tested. It provides a graphical user interface (GUI) that simplifies test design and execution, as well as a command-line interface for automation and integration with continuous integration/continuous deployment (CI/CD) pipelines.

One of the key strengths of JMeter is its extensibility; users can create custom plugins to enhance functionality, tailor test scenarios, and integrate with other tools. JMeter supports a range of testing scenarios, including load testing, stress testing, functional testing, and regression testing, making it a comprehensive solution for performance testing needs.

Key Features of JMeter:

Multi-Protocol Support: JMeter supports various protocols, including HTTP, HTTPS, FTP, JDBC, JMS, and SOAP, enabling users to test a wide range of applications and services.

User-Friendly GUI: The intuitive graphical interface allows users to design and configure tests easily, providing a visual representation of the testing process.

Scalability: JMeter can simulate thousands of concurrent users, making it suitable for load testing applications under high traffic conditions.

Detailed Reporting: JMeter generates comprehensive reports and graphs that provide insights into performance metrics, helping users analyze test results effectively.

Extensibility: JMeter allows users to create custom samplers, listeners, and functions to enhance testing capabilities and integrate with other tools.

Distributed Testing: JMeter supports distributed testing, enabling users to run tests across multiple machines to generate higher loads and simulate real-world traffic conditions.

Overview of Locust

Locust is an open-source load testing tool that enables users to define and execute load tests using Python code. It is designed to be developer-friendly, providing a simple and flexible framework for creating test scenarios that simulate user behavior. Locust's intuitive approach allows users to focus on writing test scripts in Python, making it accessible for both testers and developers.

One of Locust's primary strengths is its ability to scale effortlessly. It can generate a significant load from a single machine or scale across multiple machines to simulate thousands or even millions of concurrent users. This capability makes Locust a powerful tool for testing web applications and APIs, particularly in cloud-based environments.

Key Features of Locust:

Python-Based Test Scripts: Locust uses Python for defining user behavior, allowing users to leverage their programming skills to create complex test scenarios easily.

Web-Based User Interface: Locust provides a web-based UI for monitoring test execution in real-time. Users can start and stop tests, view statistics, and monitor system performance during testing.

Scalability: Locust can distribute load generation across multiple machines, enabling users to simulate large-scale user traffic without significant infrastructure overhead.

Realistic User Simulation: Locust allows users to define user behavior using simple Python functions, enabling the simulation of real user interactions with the application.

Detailed Metrics Reporting: Locust provides detailed statistics on key performance metrics, including response times, request counts, and failure rates, helping users analyze test results effectively.

Integration with Other Tools: Locust can easily integrate with CI/CD pipelines and other testing frameworks, enhancing its versatility in modern software development environments.

Key Differences Between JMeter and Locust

While both JMeter and Locust are powerful tools for load testing, they differ significantly in their approach, capabilities, and user experience. Understanding these differences is essential for choosing the right tool for specific testing needs.

Scripting Language:

JMeter: Users design test scenarios using a graphical user interface, making it easy for non-developers to create tests without programming knowledge. However, advanced users can write custom scripts using Groovy or Java for more complex scenarios.

Locust: Locust requires users to write test scripts in Python, making it more suitable for users with programming experience. This flexibility allows for more complex user behavior simulation but may present a learning curve for non-technical users.

User Interface:

JMeter: JMeter features a comprehensive GUI for test design and execution, providing users with visual representations of test elements. This interface can become complex as the number of test elements increases.

Locust: Locust has a clean and user-friendly web interface for monitoring tests in real time. Users can start, stop, and monitor tests without navigating a complex GUI.

Performance and Scalability:

JMeter: JMeter is capable of simulating a large number of users from a single instance. However, for distributed testing, users need to set up master-slave configurations, which can be complex to configure.

Locust: Locust is designed for scalability and can distribute load generation across multiple machines seamlessly. It can easily scale to simulate thousands of users without significant infrastructure overhead.

Reporting and Metrics:

JMeter: JMeter generates detailed reports and graphs during and after test execution, providing comprehensive insights into performance metrics. Users can customize reporting through various listeners.

Locust: Locust provides real-time statistics during test execution through its web interface, including response times, request counts, and error rates. While detailed reporting capabilities are available, users may need to leverage additional tools for comprehensive post-test reporting.

Use Cases:

JMeter: JMeter is ideal for testing web applications, APIs, and databases, making it a versatile choice for various performance testing scenarios. Its support for multiple protocols allows users to conduct diverse tests.

Locust: Locust excels in scenarios where realistic user behavior needs to be simulated, especially in web applications and APIs. Its Python-based scripting makes it suitable for testing applications developed in Python or where developers want to create complex user workflows.

Choosing the Right Tool for Load Testing

Choosing between JMeter and Locust depends on several factors, including the specific requirements of the application being tested, the skill level of the testing team, and the desired complexity of the test scenarios. Here are some considerations to help guide the decision-making process:

Team Skillset: If the testing team has strong programming skills and is comfortable with Python, Locust may be a better fit due to its flexibility in defining user behavior. Conversely, if the team prefers a graphical interface and lacks programming experience, JMeter's GUI may be more accessible.

Testing Requirements: For applications requiring support for multiple protocols and more extensive test scenarios, JMeter's versatility can be advantageous. However, for applications where user behavior simulation is critical, Locust's Python-based scripting may provide a better solution.

Scalability Needs: If the testing team anticipates needing to simulate a large number of users, Locust's scalability features make it an appealing option. On the other hand, if the team plans to run smaller-scale tests, JMeter's capabilities may suffice.

Integration and Automation: Consider how well each tool integrates with existing CI/CD pipelines and testing frameworks. Both JMeter and Locust offer integration capabilities, but the ease of integration may vary depending on the specific tools in use.

Reporting Requirements: Evaluate the reporting and metrics requirements for the testing process. JMeter offers extensive reporting capabilities, while Locust provides real-time statistics during tests but may require additional tools for detailed reporting after test execution.

In summary, both JMeter and Locust are powerful load testing tools that cater to different user needs and testing scenarios. By understanding their features, capabilities, and key differences, teams can make informed decisions on which tool is best suited for their performance testing requirements. Selecting the right tool is essential for effectively simulating user traffic, identifying performance bottlenecks, and optimizing application performance for scalable web and API services.

Chapter 4: Setting Up JMeter for Load Testing

Installing JMeter

Setting up JMeter for load testing involves several straightforward steps, enabling users to start creating and executing performance tests efficiently. Here's a detailed guide to installing JMeter on various operating systems, including prerequisites and configuration considerations.

System Requirements:

Before installing JMeter, ensure that your system meets the minimum requirements. JMeter is a Java application, so you need to have Java Development Kit (JDK) installed on your machine. It's recommended to use JDK 8 or later. Check the official JMeter documentation for specific version requirements.

Ensure that you have adequate system resources available. For load testing, JMeter may require significant CPU and memory, especially when simulating a large number of virtual users.

Download JMeter:

Visit the official Apache JMeter website at https://jmeter.apache.org/.

Navigate to the "Download" section and choose the latest stable version of JMeter. Download the binary distribution (usually a .zip or .tgz file) appropriate for your operating system.

Installing JMeter:

For Windows:

Extract the downloaded .zip file to a directory of your choice (e.g., C:\Apache\JMeter).

Navigate to the bin directory within the extracted folder.

Run jmeter.bat to launch the JMeter GUI.

For macOS:

Extract the downloaded .tgz file.

Open a terminal and navigate to the bin directory of the extracted folder.

Execute the command sh jmeter to start the JMeter GUI.

For Linux:

Extract the downloaded .tgz file using a command like tar -xzf apache-jmeter-x.x.tgz.

Open a terminal and navigate to the bin directory.

Run the command ./jmeter to start JMeter.

Configuring Environment Variables:

It may be beneficial to set environment variables for Java and JMeter. This step ensures that JMeter can easily locate the Java executable and improve usability.

For Windows, you can add the JDK and JMeter bin paths to the PATH environment variable. For example: arduino

```
setx        PATH        "%PATH%;C:\Program
Files\Java\jdk1.8.0_241\bin;C:\Apache\JMeter\bin"
```

For macOS and Linux, you can add the following lines to your .bash_profile or .bashrc: bash

```
export
JAVA_HOME=/Library/Java/JavaVirtualMachines/jdk1.8.
0_241.jdk/Contents/Home
export PATH=$PATH:/path/to/jmeter/bin
```

Verifying the Installation:

To verify that JMeter is installed correctly, launch the GUI and navigate to "Help" > "About." Ensure that the version number and details appear as expected. You can also run jmeter -v in the command line to display the version information.

Configuring JMeter for Load Testing

Once JMeter is installed, configuring it for load testing is the next critical step. This involves setting up test plans, adding necessary elements, and adjusting configurations to align with testing objectives.

Creating a Test Plan:

A test plan is the blueprint for your load test. It defines what to test, how to test it, and how to collect results. To create a new test plan, click on "File" > "New" in the JMeter GUI.

In the "Test Plan" tree, right-click on the "Test Plan" node and select "Add" > "Thread (Users)" > "Thread Group." The thread group represents a set of virtual users who will execute the defined actions.

Configuring the Thread Group:

Within the thread group, you can define several parameters:

Number of Threads (Users): This parameter specifies how many virtual users will be simulated during the test.

Ramp-Up Period: This defines the time (in seconds) over which JMeter will gradually start all the threads. For example, if you have 10 threads and set a ramp-up period of 10 seconds, JMeter will start one thread per second.

Loop Count: This defines how many times the test will run for each thread. You can set it to a fixed number or select "Forever" for continuous testing.

Adding Samplers:

Samplers are the elements that define the requests sent to the server. Right-click on the "Thread Group" node and select "Add" > "Sampler" > "HTTP Request."

In the HTTP Request sampler, specify the server name or IP address, port number, and the path for the request. This is where you define what actions the virtual users will perform on your application (e.g., loading a webpage, calling an API endpoint).

Configuring Listeners:

Listeners are used to gather and display results from your test. Right-click on the "Thread Group" node and select "Add" > "Listener" > "View Results Tree" or "Aggregate Report."

The "View Results Tree" listener displays detailed information about each request, while the "Aggregate Report" provides a summary of key metrics.

Setting Up Configuration Elements:

Configuration elements allow you to configure various parameters for your test, such as HTTP headers, user agents, and cookie handling. Right-click on the "Thread Group" node and select "Add" > "Config Element" to add relevant configurations.

For example, you can add an "HTTP Header Manager" to set headers for your requests, such as content types and authorization tokens.

Setting Up Timers:

Timers introduce delays between requests to simulate real user behavior. Right-click on the "Thread Group" node and select "Add" > "Timer" > "Constant Timer" to add a delay between requests.

Parameterization:

To make your tests more realistic, consider parameterizing input values. You can use "CSV Data Set Config" to read data from a CSV file, allowing each virtual user to use unique data during the test.

Configuring Test Execution:

Before running the test, you may want to adjust JMeter's properties to optimize performance. This can include increasing the number of threads and setting heap memory allocation. To do this, navigate to the bin directory, open the jmeter.properties file, and adjust relevant parameters.

Running Your First Load Test

With the test plan and configurations set up, you are ready to execute your first load test in JMeter.

Saving the Test Plan:

Before running the test, save your test plan by clicking "File" > "Save As" and choosing an appropriate location and file name.

Executing the Test:

Click the green "Start" button (or press Ctrl + R) to initiate the test. JMeter will simulate the defined number of virtual users and execute the configured requests.

Monitor the test execution in real-time through the listeners you added. The "View Results Tree" listener will show the details of each request and response, while the "Aggregate Report" will summarize performance metrics.

Analyzing Test Results:

Once the test is completed, analyze the results displayed in the listeners. Pay attention to key metrics such as response times, throughput, and error rates.

Identify any performance bottlenecks or issues that arise during testing. You can use this information to refine your application, optimize server configurations, or adjust your test scenarios.

Exporting Results:

JMeter allows you to export test results for further analysis. Right-click on the listener and choose "Save As" to export results in various formats (e.g., CSV or XML).

Iterating on Tests:

Load testing is an iterative process. Use insights gained from your initial tests to refine your test plan, adjust configurations, and run additional tests as needed. By continuously testing and refining, you can ensure that your application performs optimally under varying load conditions.

Best Practices for Using JMeter

As you begin using JMeter for load testing, consider the following best practices to enhance your testing process:

Use Realistic Load Patterns: When designing your tests, aim to simulate real user behavior. Consider factors such as concurrent users, ramp-up times, and think times to create more accurate load scenarios.

Keep Tests Modular: Break your test plans into modular components. This approach allows for easier maintenance, reuse of components, and better organization of complex test scenarios.

Monitor Server Performance: In addition to testing the application itself, monitor server performance during load tests. Use monitoring tools to track resource utilization (CPU, memory, disk I/O) to identify potential bottlenecks.

Run Tests in a Staging Environment: Conduct load tests in a staging or pre-production environment that mirrors your production setup. This practice helps ensure that test results are relevant and applicable to real-world scenarios.

Validate Results with Multiple Runs: Perform multiple test runs to validate results and identify inconsistencies. This approach helps eliminate anomalies and provides a clearer picture of application performance.

By following these guidelines and utilizing JMeter effectively, you can establish a robust load testing process that identifies performance bottlenecks, optimizes application performance, and enhances user experience.

Chapter 5: Setting Up Locust for Load Testing

Introduction to Locust

Locust is an open-source load testing tool that allows users to simulate millions of concurrent users on web applications. Its user-friendly interface and Python-based scripting make it a popular choice among developers and testers for performance testing. This chapter will explore how to set up Locust for load testing, covering installation, configuration, and executing your first load test.

Installing Locust

Setting up Locust is straightforward, particularly for those familiar with Python. Follow these steps to install Locust on various operating systems.

System Requirements:

Locust requires Python 3.6 or later. Ensure you have Python installed on your system. You can download Python from the official website: https://www.python.org/downloads/.

Installing Locust via Pip:

The easiest way to install Locust is by using the Python package manager, pip. Open a terminal or command prompt and execute the following command: bash

```
pip install locust
```

This command will download and install the latest version of Locust along with its dependencies.

Verifying the Installation:

To verify that Locust is installed correctly, run the following command in your terminal: bash

```
locust --version
```

This command should return the installed version of Locust, confirming that the installation was successful.

Setting Up a Virtual Environment (Optional):

It is a good practice to use a virtual environment to isolate your project dependencies. You can create a virtual environment using the following commands: bash

```
python -m venv locust_env
source locust_env/bin/activate    # On Windows, use
locust_env\Scripts\activate
```

After activating the virtual environment, you can install Locust within it.

Creating a Basic Load Test with Locust

Once Locust is installed, the next step is to create a simple load test script. Locust uses a Python-based approach, allowing users to define user behavior through classes and methods.

Understanding the Locust File Structure:

A Locust load test script is a Python file that defines user behavior. By convention, the file is named locustfile.py. This file will contain the classes and methods that simulate user interactions with your application.

Defining User Behavior:

To create a basic load test, you need to define a class that inherits from HttpUser. This class represents a user who will perform actions on your application. Here is a simple example of a Locust script:

```python
from locust import HttpUser, TaskSet, task

class UserBehavior(TaskSet):
    @task
    def load_home_page(self):
        self.client.get("/")  # Simulate a GET request to the home page

    @task
    def load_about_page(self):
```

```python
        self.client.get("/about")  # Simulate a GET request to the
        about page

class WebsiteUser(HttpUser):
    tasks = {UserBehavior: 1}  # Assign the UserBehavior
    class to the user
    min_wait = 5000  # Minimum wait time between tasks (in
    milliseconds)
    max_wait = 15000  # Maximum wait time between tasks
    (in milliseconds)
```

Script Explanation:

In the above script, we import necessary modules from Locust.

UserBehavior is a class that defines the tasks that the simulated user will perform. The @task decorator marks methods as tasks that will be executed by the user.

The WebsiteUser class defines the user type and assigns the UserBehavior class. The min_wait and max_wait attributes specify the wait time between tasks, simulating realistic user behavior.

Running Your Load Test:

To run the load test, navigate to the directory containing your locustfile.py in the terminal. Then, execute the following command:
bash
```
locust -f locustfile.py --host=http://yourwebsite.com
```

43

Replace http://yourwebsite.com with the target URL of your application.

Accessing the Locust Web Interface:

Once you run the command, Locust will start a web server. By default, the web interface is accessible at http://localhost:8089.

Open your web browser and navigate to this URL to access the Locust web interface.

Configuring the Load Test:

In the Locust web interface, you can specify the number of users to simulate and the hatch rate (the number of users to start per second).

Enter the desired values in the respective fields and click the "Start swarming" button to initiate the load test.

Monitoring the Load Test:

As the test runs, you can monitor real-time metrics such as request per second, response times, and the number of users currently active.

The interface provides detailed statistics, including the number of successful and failed requests, enabling you to quickly identify performance issues.

Stopping the Load Test:

To stop the load test, simply click the "Stop" button in the web interface. Locust will halt the test and display the final statistics.

Advanced Configuration Options

Once you have a basic load test up and running, you can explore more advanced features in Locust to enhance your testing capabilities.

Using Multiple Tasks:

You can define multiple tasks within your UserBehavior class to simulate a variety of user actions. This helps create a more realistic testing scenario. For instance, you can add additional tasks for logging in, searching for products, or completing a purchase.

```python
class UserBehavior(TaskSet):
@task
def load_home_page(self):
self.client.get("/")

@task
def load_product_page(self):
self.client.get("/products/1")

@task
def user_login(self):
self.client.post("/login", {"username": "user", "password": "pass"})
```

Weighting Tasks:

To simulate varying frequencies of tasks, you can assign weights to them. Higher weight values increase the likelihood of a task being executed. For example:

python
```
class UserBehavior(TaskSet):
@task(2)  # This task will be executed twice as often as the others
def load_home_page(self):
self.client.get("/")

@task(1)
def load_about_page(self):
self.client.get("/about")
```

Setting Up User Classes:

You can define multiple user classes with different behaviors and weights, allowing you to simulate various user roles interacting with your application.

python
```
class AdminUser(HttpUser):
tasks = {AdminBehavior: 1}
min_wait = 1000
max_wait = 5000
```

Parameterization:

Locust supports parameterization through CSV or JSON files. You can use the between method in your user classes to set dynamic wait times or load user data from external sources.

Using Event Listeners:

Locust provides event listeners to extend functionality and add custom behavior during the test execution. You can hook into events like user start, request success, or request failure to log information or take specific actions.

```python
from locust import events

@events.request.add_listener
def log_request(request_type, name, response_time, response_length, **kwargs):
    print(f"Request {name} took {response_time} ms")
```

Analyzing Results

Locust provides real-time metrics and detailed reports, which are essential for analyzing performance and identifying bottlenecks.

Real-Time Metrics:

The web interface displays key performance indicators such as:

Requests per Second (RPS): Indicates how many requests are being processed by the server.

Average Response Time: The average time taken to respond to requests.

Error Rate: The percentage of requests that resulted in errors.

Exporting Results:

Locust allows you to export the test results for further analysis. You can use the built-in logging feature to save results to a CSV file or integrate with third-party monitoring tools to visualize performance data.

Using Third-Party Tools for Analysis:

Integrate Locust with tools like Grafana or Prometheus for advanced data visualization and monitoring. This combination can provide insightful dashboards and alerting mechanisms based on load test performance metrics.

Iterating on Test Scenarios:

Based on the results obtained, refine your test scenarios to address any performance issues. Adjust user behavior, increase the number of simulated users, or modify request parameters to simulate different load conditions.

Best Practices for Using Locust

To maximize the effectiveness of Locust for load testing, consider the following best practices:

Use Realistic User Behavior:

Simulate real-world user interactions as closely as possible to obtain meaningful results. Consider user paths, session times, and think times.

Test in a Controlled Environment:

Perform load tests in a controlled environment that mimics production settings to ensure the accuracy and relevance of results.

Run Multiple Test Iterations:

Conduct multiple iterations of load tests to validate results and identify patterns. This practice helps eliminate anomalies and ensures reliability.

Monitor Resource Utilization:

In addition to application performance metrics, monitor server resource utilization (CPU, memory, disk I/O) to identify potential bottlenecks.

Document and Share Findings:

Maintain documentation of test scenarios, configurations, and results. Sharing insights with development and operations teams can facilitate performance improvements.

Setting up Locust for load testing is an essential step in ensuring the performance and scalability of web applications. By following the steps outlined in this chapter, you can create effective load tests that simulate real user behavior, identify performance issues, and gather valuable insights for optimization. With its powerful features and flexibility, Locust is a valuable tool for developers and testers alike, enabling them to deliver high-quality applications that can withstand the demands of real-world usage.

Chapter 6: Configuring JMeter for Load Testing

Introduction to JMeter

Apache JMeter is a popular open-source tool designed for performance testing, particularly for web applications. It is widely used for load testing, functional testing, and performance measurement. JMeter supports various protocols, including HTTP, HTTPS, SOAP, REST, and more, making it a versatile choice for testing both web and API services. In this chapter, we will explore how to configure JMeter for load testing, covering installation, test plan creation, and executing load tests.

Installing JMeter

Setting up JMeter involves downloading the software and ensuring that your environment is ready for use.

System Requirements:

JMeter requires Java 8 or later. Before installing JMeter, make sure that Java is installed on your machine. You can verify this by running the following command in your terminal or command prompt: bash

```
java -version
```

Downloading JMeter:

Visit the official Apache JMeter website at https://jmeter.apache.org/downloads.html and download the latest binary release in zip or tgz format.

Extracting the Files:

After downloading, extract the contents of the zip or tgz file to a directory of your choice. This will create a folder named apache-jmeter-x.x (where x.x is the version number).

Launching JMeter:

Navigate to the bin directory within the extracted JMeter folder and execute the jmeter.bat file (Windows) or jmeter file (Linux/Mac) to launch the JMeter GUI.

Verifying the Installation:

Upon launching, the JMeter GUI should open, confirming that the installation was successful.

Creating a Basic Load Test Plan

A load test in JMeter is defined through a test plan, which contains all the configurations and components required for the test. Here's how to create a basic load test plan:

Creating a New Test Plan:

Open JMeter and select File > New to create a new test plan. A test plan serves as the container for your test components.

Naming Your Test Plan:

Right-click on the Test Plan node in the left panel, select Rename, and give your test plan a descriptive name (e.g., "Basic Load Test").

Adding Thread Groups:

A thread group represents a group of virtual users (threads) that will execute the test. To add a thread group:

Right-click on the Test Plan node.

Select Add > Threads (Users) > Thread Group.

In the Thread Group settings, configure the following parameters:

Number of Threads (users): The number of concurrent users to simulate.

Ramp-Up Period (seconds): The time it takes for all threads to start.

Loop Count: The number of times to execute the test.

Adding HTTP Request Samplers:

To simulate requests to your application, add HTTP request samplers within the thread group:

Right-click on the Thread Group node.

Select Add > Sampler > HTTP Request.

In the HTTP Request settings, configure the following:

Server Name or IP: Enter the domain name or IP address of the server you are testing.

HTTP Method: Choose the request method (GET, POST, etc.).

Path: Specify the endpoint you want to test (e.g., /api/v1/resource).

Configuring Listeners:

Listeners allow you to view and analyze the results of your tests. To add a listener:

Right-click on the Thread Group node.

Select Add > Listener > View Results Tree or Summary Report.

Listeners will collect and display data such as response times, request counts, and success rates.

Setting Up Assertions (Optional):

Assertions enable you to validate responses from the server. To add an assertion:

Right-click on the HTTP Request sampler.

Select Add > Assertions > Response Assertion.

In the Response Assertion settings, configure the criteria you want to test (e.g., response code, response body).

Saving Your Test Plan:

Once your test plan is configured, save it by selecting File > Save As and choose a location on your machine.

Executing Your Load Test

With the test plan configured, you are ready to execute your load test. Follow these steps to run your test and analyze the results:

Starting the Test:

Click the green "Start" button in the JMeter toolbar to begin the load test. JMeter will start simulating the configured number of users and execute the specified requests.

Monitoring Test Execution:

During the test, you can monitor the performance metrics in real-time through the listeners you added. The View Results Tree listener will display the requests being executed and their responses.

Stopping the Test:

To stop the test before it completes, click the red "Stop" button in the toolbar. JMeter will halt all running threads and display the collected results up to that point.

Analyzing Results:

After stopping the test, review the results in the listeners. The Summary Report will provide key metrics such as:

Average Response Time: The average time taken for requests to complete.

Total Number of Samples: The total requests made during the test.

Error Percentage: The percentage of failed requests.

Exporting Results:

You can export the results for further analysis by right-clicking on a listener and selecting the export option. This feature is useful for creating reports and sharing findings with stakeholders.

Advanced JMeter Configurations

Once you have mastered the basics, you can explore advanced configurations in JMeter to enhance your load testing capabilities.

Using CSV Data Set Config:

To simulate realistic user behavior, you can use a CSV Data Set Config to parameterize your requests with different user credentials or input data.

Right-click on the Thread Group node.

Select Add > Config Element > CSV Data Set Config.

In the settings, specify the path to your CSV file and define variable names that correspond to the columns in the file. This allows you to dynamically assign values to your HTTP requests.

Configuring Timers:

Timers help to simulate think times between requests. To add a timer:

Right-click on the Thread Group node.

Select Add > Timer > Constant Timer or Gaussian Random Timer.

Set the delay time to simulate realistic user interactions.

Implementing Logic Controllers:

Logic controllers allow you to control the flow of the test and manage how requests are executed. Examples include:

If Controller: Executes child requests only if a specific condition is met.

Loop Controller: Repeats child requests a specified number of times.

Random Controller: Randomly selects child requests to execute.

Setting Up Distributed Testing:

For large-scale load testing, JMeter supports distributed testing where multiple machines can be used to simulate a high number of users.

This requires setting up one master node and multiple slave nodes. You will need to configure each slave with the same test plan and execute them from the master.

Using Plugins:

The JMeter Plugins Manager allows you to extend JMeter's functionality with additional features such as custom listeners, samplers, and report generation tools.

Install the Plugins Manager by downloading the JAR file from the JMeter Plugins website and placing it in the lib/ext directory of your JMeter installation.

Configuring Performance Metrics:

You can use the JMeter Dashboard to create reports that visualize performance metrics over time. The dashboard provides graphical representations of response times, throughput, and error rates, making it easier to identify performance bottlenecks.

Best Practices for Using JMeter

To ensure effective load testing with JMeter, adhere to the following best practices:

Design Realistic User Scenarios:

Simulate user journeys accurately to obtain meaningful results. Consider typical user interactions, session lengths, and usage patterns.

Use Descriptive Names:

Name your test plans, thread groups, and samplers descriptively to maintain clarity, especially when collaborating with other team members.

Conduct Test Iterations:

Run multiple iterations of your load tests to validate results and account for variability. Analyze trends over time rather than relying on a single test run.

Monitor Resource Utilization:

Monitor server metrics (CPU, memory, network) during load tests to identify potential bottlenecks in infrastructure.

Document Test Plans:

Maintain documentation of test plans, configurations, and results. This documentation will be valuable for future reference and sharing insights with stakeholders.

Review and Optimize Test Plans:

Regularly review and optimize your test plans to ensure they remain relevant and effective as your application evolves.

Configuring JMeter for load testing is a critical step in evaluating the performance and scalability of web applications. By following the steps outlined in this chapter, you can create effective load tests that simulate real user behavior, identify performance issues, and gather valuable insights for optimization. JMeter's extensive features and capabilities make it a powerful tool for developers and testers, enabling them to deliver high-quality applications that can handle the demands of real-world usage.

Chapter 7: Load Testing Strategies with JMeter and Locust

Understanding Load Testing Strategies

Load testing is a crucial aspect of performance engineering, aimed at assessing how a system behaves under expected and peak load conditions. Choosing the right load testing strategy is essential for obtaining accurate insights into the performance of web applications and APIs. This chapter will explore various load testing strategies using JMeter and Locust, focusing on their implementation, advantages, and best practices.

Types of Load Testing Strategies

Baseline Testing:

Baseline testing establishes a performance benchmark by testing the application under normal load conditions. It serves as a reference point for future testing.

Implementation:

Configure a test plan in JMeter or Locust that simulates a typical user load based on historical usage data.

Collect metrics such as response times, throughput, and error rates to establish baseline performance metrics.

Advantages:

Provides a clear picture of the application's performance under expected usage.

Facilitates comparison with future test results to identify performance degradation or improvements.

Stress Testing:

Stress testing evaluates the application's behavior under extreme load conditions, pushing the system beyond its limits to identify breaking points and failure modes.

Implementation:

Gradually increase the number of virtual users in JMeter or Locust until the system reaches its maximum capacity or fails.

Monitor system metrics such as CPU and memory usage during the test.

Advantages:

Helps identify performance bottlenecks and failure points that may not be evident under normal conditions.

Assists in understanding how the system recovers from failures.

Spike Testing:

Spike testing simulates sudden and extreme increases in load, allowing testers to assess how the system responds to abrupt traffic spikes.

Implementation:

Configure JMeter or Locust to simulate a rapid increase in virtual users over a short period, followed by a sudden drop in load.

Analyze how the application behaves during the spike and how quickly it recovers.

Advantages:

Reveals vulnerabilities in handling unexpected traffic surges.

Provides insights into system resilience and recovery capabilities.

Endurance Testing:

Endurance testing, also known as soak testing, assesses the system's performance over an extended period under a specified load. It aims to identify issues that may arise over time, such as memory leaks and resource exhaustion.

Implementation:

Set up a long-duration test in JMeter or Locust with a stable load that mimics continuous usage.

Monitor system metrics and application behavior throughout the testing period.

Advantages:

Identifies potential long-term performance issues that may not be apparent in shorter tests.

Validates the system's stability and resource management over time.

Concurrency Testing:

Concurrency testing evaluates how well the application handles simultaneous requests from multiple users. It aims to identify issues related to data consistency, locking, and resource contention.

Implementation:

Design a test in JMeter or Locust that simulates multiple users performing concurrent operations on shared resources.

Analyze response times and error rates to identify any concurrency-related issues.

Advantages:

Helps identify race conditions and data integrity issues.

Assesses the system's ability to manage concurrent access effectively.

Configuration Testing:

Configuration testing evaluates the application's performance under various configurations, such as different hardware setups, network conditions, or software environments.

Implementation:

Use JMeter or Locust to test the application in different configurations by adjusting parameters such as the number of threads, server capacity, or network bandwidth.

Collect performance metrics for each configuration to assess the impact on performance.

Advantages:

Helps optimize the application for different environments and conditions.

Assists in identifying the optimal configuration for performance.

Implementing Load Testing Strategies with JMeter

Baseline Testing with JMeter:

Create a test plan that simulates normal user load based on historical data.

Use a Thread Group with a fixed number of threads to represent the expected user load.

Execute the test and collect baseline performance metrics using listeners such as "Summary Report" and "View Results Tree."

Stress Testing with JMeter:

Set up a test plan with a Thread Group configured for a higher number of threads than the system is expected to handle.

Gradually increase the thread count to identify the point at which the system fails or performance degrades significantly.

Monitor server resource utilization during the test to gain insights into performance bottlenecks.

Spike Testing with JMeter:

Configure a Thread Group that rapidly increases the number of threads to simulate a sudden spike in user traffic.

Use a "Constant Throughput Timer" to control the request rate during the test.

Analyze how the system handles the sudden load increase and its recovery behavior after the spike.

Endurance Testing with JMeter:

Create a long-duration test plan that runs for several hours, simulating a stable user load.

Utilize "Duration" and "Loop Count" settings in the Thread Group to control the test length.

Monitor performance metrics over time to identify any gradual performance degradation.

Concurrency Testing with JMeter:

Design a test plan that simulates multiple users accessing shared resources concurrently.

Configure multiple Thread Groups, each representing different user actions (e.g., creating, reading, updating).

Analyze response times and error rates to identify issues related to data contention.

Configuration Testing with JMeter:

Develop multiple test plans with different configurations and parameters.

Compare performance metrics across different configurations to identify the optimal setup for your application.

Implementing Load Testing Strategies with Locust

Baseline Testing with Locust:

Define a user behavior script in Locust that simulates normal user actions.

Set the number of users to the expected baseline load and execute the test.

Collect performance metrics using Locust's built-in web UI for real-time monitoring.

Stress Testing with Locust:

Create a user behavior script that simulates more users than the system can handle.

Gradually ramp up the user count to identify the breaking point of the system.

Monitor system performance metrics during the test to gain insights into stress limits.

Spike Testing with Locust:

Design a user behavior script that simulates a sudden increase in users over a short period.

Use the Locust web UI to control the number of users dynamically during the test.

Analyze how the system responds to the sudden spike in traffic.

Endurance Testing with Locust:

Set up a long-running test using Locust to simulate continuous user load for several hours.

Use the web UI to monitor real-time performance metrics throughout the testing period.

Analyze metrics over time to identify any long-term performance issues.

Concurrency Testing with Locust:

Develop a user behavior script that simulates concurrent actions from multiple users.

Configure Locust to run multiple instances of the script simultaneously.

Assess the system's ability to handle concurrent requests effectively.

Configuration Testing with Locust:

Create multiple user behavior scripts with different configurations.

Compare performance metrics across different setups to identify optimal configurations.

Best Practices for Load Testing Strategies

Define Clear Objectives:

Establish clear testing goals and metrics to assess performance effectively. Knowing what you want to achieve will guide your testing approach.

Choose the Right Strategy:

Select the most appropriate load testing strategy based on your objectives and application requirements. Different scenarios may require different approaches.

Involve Stakeholders:

Collaborate with development and operations teams to ensure that testing aligns with business needs and application architecture.

Automate Tests Where Possible:

Automate load tests to enable continuous performance testing as part of your CI/CD pipeline. This approach allows for regular performance assessments without manual intervention.

Analyze Results Thoroughly:

Take the time to analyze test results carefully. Look for patterns, trends, and correlations in performance metrics to identify potential issues.

Document Findings:

Maintain documentation of test plans, configurations, and results to ensure that insights are readily available for future reference.

Iterate and Improve:

Load testing should be an iterative process. Use insights from previous tests to refine test plans, enhance configurations, and improve application performance.

Consider Real-World Conditions:

Simulate real-world conditions as closely as possible. Use realistic user behavior, network conditions, and hardware configurations to obtain meaningful results.

Choosing the right load testing strategy is essential for accurately assessing application performance and identifying potential bottlenecks. By implementing various load testing strategies with JMeter and Locust, you can gain valuable insights into how your application performs under different load conditions. This understanding is crucial for optimizing performance, ensuring scalability, and delivering high-quality web and API services.

Chapter 8: Analyzing Load Test Results with JMeter and Locust

Importance of Analyzing Load Test Results

Analyzing load test results is a critical step in the performance testing lifecycle. It allows teams to understand how their applications respond under various load conditions and to identify performance bottlenecks. The insights derived from these analyses can inform decisions about optimization, resource allocation, and future testing strategies. This chapter will cover the methodologies for analyzing load test results using JMeter and Locust, focusing on key metrics, interpretation techniques, and visualization methods.

Key Metrics for Analysis

Response Time:

Definition: The time taken by the server to respond to a request from a client. It is a crucial metric that reflects the performance perceived by the end user.

Analysis:

Examine the average response time, maximum and minimum response times, and percentiles (e.g., 90th, 95th).

Identify trends over time, especially during peak load periods. A sharp increase in response time can indicate performance degradation or bottlenecks.

Throughput:

Definition: The number of requests processed by the application over a specific time period, usually measured in requests per second (RPS).

Analysis:

Assess throughput against response time to understand how increased load impacts the system's ability to handle requests.

Evaluate if the throughput meets the expected benchmarks set during baseline testing.

Error Rate:

Definition: The percentage of requests that result in errors, which can include HTTP errors (like 404, 500) or application-specific failures.

Analysis:

Calculate the error rate and identify patterns. A sudden spike in error rates can indicate issues such as resource exhaustion or misconfigurations.

Correlate error rates with response times and throughput to gain insights into the causes of failures.

Resource Utilization:

Definition: Metrics related to CPU, memory, disk I/O, and network usage on the server side during load tests.

Analysis:

Monitor resource utilization to identify potential bottlenecks. High CPU or memory usage can indicate that the application is reaching its limits.

Analyze the relationship between resource utilization and application performance metrics to understand how resources impact performance.

Latency:

Definition: The delay experienced in data transmission over the network, which can be a significant factor in response times.

Analysis:

Measure both client-side and server-side latency to identify where delays occur. High latency can indicate network issues, while server-side latency reflects application performance.

Assess how latency varies under different load conditions to determine the impact on user experience.

Connection Time:

Definition: The time taken to establish a connection to the server before a request is sent.

Analysis:

Monitor connection times, especially under high load scenarios. Increasing connection times may indicate server overload or network issues.

Consider connection pooling and server configurations to improve connection time performance.

Techniques for Analyzing Load Test Results

Statistical Analysis:

Use statistical methods to summarize and interpret load test data. Calculate averages, percentiles, standard deviations, and trends over time.

Identify outliers in the data that may indicate unusual performance issues or unexpected behavior.

Comparative Analysis:

Compare results across different test scenarios, configurations, or application versions. This approach helps identify the impact of changes made to the application or environment.

Use baseline performance metrics as reference points for comparison to gauge improvements or regressions.

Correlation Analysis:

Investigate relationships between different metrics. For instance, analyze how increased load affects response time and error rates.

Utilize tools to visualize correlations, such as scatter plots or heat maps, to identify patterns and anomalies in the data.

Root Cause Analysis (RCA):

Conduct a systematic examination of performance issues to determine their root causes. RCA involves investigating potential bottlenecks in the application, infrastructure, or configurations.

Use logs, monitoring tools, and system metrics to pinpoint issues contributing to performance degradation.

Trend Analysis:

Track performance metrics over time to identify trends, patterns, or recurring issues. This analysis helps in understanding the long-term performance characteristics of the application.

Use time-series graphs to visualize changes in response times, throughput, and error rates across different load scenarios.

Visualizing Load Test Results

Graphs and Charts:

Use graphs and charts to present key metrics clearly. Common visualizations include:

Line Charts: Effective for displaying trends over time, such as response time or throughput.

Bar Charts: Useful for comparing metrics across different test scenarios or configurations.

Pie Charts: Can illustrate the distribution of error types or resource usage.

Dashboards:

Create dashboards that aggregate key performance metrics in real time. Tools like Grafana or Kibana can visualize data from JMeter or Locust for easy monitoring and analysis.

Dashboards should provide insights into performance health, including real-time response times, error rates, and resource utilization.

Heat Maps:

Use heat maps to visualize the distribution of performance metrics, such as response times across different user scenarios or endpoints.

Heat maps can help quickly identify areas of concern, such as endpoints that consistently exhibit high response times.

Logs and Reports:

Generate detailed logs and reports that capture all relevant metrics and events during the load test. Include timestamps, response times, error details, and resource utilization metrics.

Logs can serve as a valuable reference for post-test analysis and troubleshooting.

Annotation:

Annotate graphs and charts with contextual information about test configurations, such as changes made during testing or specific events that may have impacted performance.

This additional context helps stakeholders understand performance variations and provides insights for future tests.

Tools for Analyzing Load Test Results

JMeter Listeners:

JMeter provides several built-in listeners for analyzing results, including "Summary Report," "View Results Tree," and "Aggregate Report." Each listener provides different insights and can be customized based on the analysis needs.

Use these listeners to extract performance metrics and visualize them in different formats.

Locust Web UI:

The Locust web interface provides real-time monitoring and visualization of test results. It displays key metrics, including response times, request counts, and failure rates.

Leverage the web UI for quick access to performance insights during testing.

External Reporting Tools:

Utilize external reporting tools like Grafana or Kibana to visualize performance data collected during tests. Integrate these tools with JMeter or Locust to create custom dashboards that provide insights into performance metrics.

These tools offer advanced visualization capabilities and support for various data sources.

Database or Log Analysis Tools:

Consider using database or log analysis tools like ELK (Elasticsearch, Logstash, Kibana) stack to aggregate and analyze logs generated during load testing.

These tools enable powerful querying and visualization capabilities for deeper insights into application performance.

Custom Scripts and Analysis:

Write custom scripts in programming languages like Python or R to analyze load test data. These scripts can automate the analysis process and provide tailored insights based on specific requirements.

Utilize libraries such as Pandas or Matplotlib for data manipulation and visualization in Python.

Best Practices for Analyzing Load Test Results

Establish Baselines:

Set baseline metrics during initial testing phases to facilitate future comparisons. Baselines provide reference points for evaluating performance changes over time.

Collaborate with Stakeholders:

Involve relevant stakeholders in the analysis process. Developers, QA teams, and business leaders can provide valuable insights and interpretations of test results.

Focus on User Experience:

Prioritize metrics that directly impact user experience, such as response times and error rates. Understanding how performance affects users is crucial for making informed decisions.

Document Findings:

Keep detailed documentation of test results, analyses, and conclusions. This documentation serves as a reference for future tests and helps maintain knowledge continuity.

Iterate and Optimize:

Use insights from load test analyses to iterate on application performance. Continuously optimize based on findings to improve overall system efficiency.

Regularly Review Performance:

Establish a routine for regular load testing and performance reviews. Frequent testing helps ensure that performance remains optimal as the application evolves.

Adjust Testing Strategies Based on Findings:

Be prepared to adjust testing strategies based on analysis outcomes. If certain performance issues are identified, consider implementing targeted tests to investigate further.

Stay Informed on Tools and Techniques:

Keep up with advancements in load testing tools and analysis techniques. The landscape is continually evolving, and staying informed will enhance your testing capabilities.

Analyzing load test results is an essential part of performance testing that provides valuable insights into application behavior under various load conditions. By focusing on key metrics, employing effective analysis techniques, and utilizing visualization tools, teams can identify performance bottlenecks, optimize application performance, and ensure a positive user experience. The methodologies discussed in this chapter equip performance engineers with the knowledge to conduct thorough analyses and make informed decisions regarding application optimization.

Chapter 9: Performance Optimization Strategies with JMeter and Locust

Understanding Performance Optimization

Performance optimization in the context of web and API services involves enhancing the speed, efficiency, and responsiveness of applications to improve user experience and resource utilization. With increasing user expectations and the growing complexity of web applications, effective performance optimization is critical for maintaining competitive advantages in today's digital landscape. This chapter will discuss various strategies for optimizing application performance using JMeter and Locust, covering both server-side and client-side optimizations, configuration adjustments, and best practices.

Key Areas of Performance Optimization

Server-Side Optimization:

Focuses on improving the backend components of an application, including database interactions, server configurations, and application logic.

Critical for enhancing response times and reducing server load under high traffic conditions.

Client-Side Optimization:

Involves enhancing front-end performance to improve load times and user interactions.

Critical for delivering a seamless user experience and reducing perceived latency.

Infrastructure Optimization:

Addresses the underlying hardware and network components that support applications.

Involves optimizing server resources, load balancing, and network configurations.

Server-Side Optimization Techniques

Database Optimization:

Indexing: Create indexes on frequently queried columns to speed up database read operations. Proper indexing can significantly reduce query response times.

Query Optimization: Analyze and optimize SQL queries to eliminate inefficient operations. Use EXPLAIN plans to understand query execution and identify bottlenecks.

Connection Pooling: Implement connection pooling to manage database connections efficiently. This approach minimizes the overhead of establishing new connections for each request.

Application Logic Optimization:

Code Profiling: Use profiling tools to analyze application code performance and identify hotspots. Optimize slow functions and methods to improve overall response times.

Caching Strategies: Implement caching mechanisms to store frequently accessed data, reducing the need for repeated database queries. Utilize in-memory caches (e.g., Redis, Memcached) for fast data retrieval.

Asynchronous Processing: Offload time-consuming tasks to background processes or queues, allowing the main application to handle user requests more efficiently.

Load Balancing:

Distribute incoming traffic across multiple server instances to prevent any single server from becoming a bottleneck. Load balancing can enhance application availability and fault tolerance.

Use strategies such as round-robin, least connections, or IP hash to distribute loads effectively.

Content Delivery Network (CDN):

Utilize a CDN to cache and deliver static assets (e.g., images, stylesheets, scripts) from locations closer to users. CDNs reduce latency and improve load times, especially for geographically dispersed audiences.

Implementing a CDN can also alleviate load on the origin server by offloading traffic.

Optimize Server Configurations:

Adjust web server configurations (e.g., Apache, Nginx) to enhance performance. This includes tuning parameters like worker processes, timeouts, and keep-alive settings.

Ensure the server has sufficient resources (CPU, RAM) to handle expected loads without performance degradation.

Microservices Architecture:

Consider adopting a microservices architecture to decouple application components. This approach allows teams to optimize individual services independently and scale them based on demand.

Client-Side Optimization Techniques

Minification and Bundling:

Minify CSS, JavaScript, and HTML files to reduce file sizes and improve load times. Bundling multiple files into a single request can also decrease the number of HTTP requests, enhancing performance.

Tools like Webpack or Gulp can automate minification and bundling processes.

Image Optimization:

Optimize images by compressing file sizes without sacrificing quality. Use appropriate formats (e.g., WebP, JPEG, PNG) and dimensions based on use cases.

Implement lazy loading for images to load them only when they are in the viewport, reducing initial load times.

Reduce HTTP Requests:

Minimize the number of HTTP requests made by the client by combining files, utilizing CSS sprites, and reducing the use of external resources.

Use resource hints (e.g., prefetching, preloading) to optimize resource loading times.

Browser Caching:

Configure browser caching for static assets to reduce load times for returning visitors. Set appropriate cache-control headers to inform browsers how long to cache resources.

Utilize techniques like service workers for advanced caching strategies in Progressive Web Applications (PWAs).

Optimize Rendering Performance:

Reduce reflows and repaints in the browser by minimizing DOM manipulations and optimizing CSS selectors. Batch updates to the DOM to improve rendering efficiency.

Use techniques like requestAnimationFrame to synchronize animations with the browser's refresh rate, providing smoother visual experiences.

Infrastructure Optimization Techniques

Vertical Scaling vs. Horizontal Scaling:

Vertical Scaling: Increase the capacity of existing servers by adding more resources (CPU, RAM). This approach is straightforward but may reach physical limitations.

Horizontal Scaling: Add more servers to distribute the load. Horizontal scaling offers greater flexibility and resilience against failures.

Network Optimization:

Optimize network configurations to reduce latency and improve throughput. Use techniques like TCP tuning, optimizing DNS resolution times, and reducing packet loss.

Implementing HTTP/2 can enhance performance by allowing multiple requests to be sent simultaneously over a single connection.

Resource Monitoring:

Use monitoring tools to track infrastructure performance, such as CPU usage, memory consumption, disk I/O, and network traffic. Proactive monitoring helps identify bottlenecks before they impact users.

Tools like Prometheus, Grafana, or New Relic can provide real-time insights into infrastructure performance.

JMeter and Locust for Performance Optimization Testing

Simulating Realistic Load:

Use JMeter and Locust to simulate realistic user traffic patterns and loads. Create scenarios that mimic actual user behavior to evaluate how optimizations impact performance under expected conditions.

Adjust the number of virtual users, ramp-up times, and think times to create accurate load test scenarios.

Conducting Performance Profiling:

Employ JMeter's built-in listeners to capture performance metrics during load tests. Analyze response times, throughput, and error rates to assess the impact of optimizations.

Use Locust's web interface to visualize real-time performance data and monitor how optimizations affect system behavior under load.

Iterative Testing:

Implement an iterative approach to performance testing. After applying optimizations, conduct load tests to evaluate the effectiveness of changes.

Use results to make informed decisions on further optimizations or adjustments required for optimal performance.

Best Practices for Performance Optimization

Establish Performance Benchmarks:

Set clear performance benchmarks during initial testing phases. This allows teams to measure the effectiveness of optimizations against predefined criteria.

Regularly Review Performance:

Conduct regular performance reviews to ensure that applications meet performance expectations over time. Continuous monitoring and optimization are key to maintaining performance as applications evolve.

Document Optimization Processes:

Maintain detailed documentation of performance optimization efforts, including methodologies, results, and lessons learned. This documentation serves as a valuable resource for future optimization initiatives.

Engage Stakeholders in Optimization Efforts:

Involve relevant stakeholders, including developers, operations teams, and business leaders, in performance optimization discussions. Collaboration ensures that optimizations align with business goals and user expectations.

Stay Informed About New Technologies:

Keep up with advancements in optimization techniques, tools, and technologies. The performance landscape is continuously evolving, and staying informed will enhance your optimization strategies.

Test in Production-like Environments:

Conduct performance tests in environments that closely mimic production to obtain accurate results. This approach helps ensure that optimizations are effective in real-world scenarios.

Prioritize User Experience:

Keep the user experience at the forefront of optimization efforts. Understand how performance impacts user satisfaction and prioritize optimizations that enhance user interactions.

Iterate Based on Feedback:

Use feedback from users and stakeholders to inform performance optimization efforts. Iterative improvements based on real user experiences can lead to meaningful enhancements.

Performance optimization is a multifaceted process that involves analyzing, refining, and enhancing various components of web and API services. By employing the strategies discussed in this chapter, teams can effectively optimize their applications for improved response times, higher throughput, and better overall user experience. Utilizing tools like JMeter and Locust enables performance engineers to simulate realistic user loads, measure performance, and implement optimizations effectively, ensuring applications remain competitive and efficient in today's demanding environment.

Chapter 10: Monitoring and Analyzing Performance Metrics

The Importance of Performance Monitoring

Monitoring and analyzing performance metrics is crucial for maintaining the health of web applications and APIs. Performance monitoring enables organizations to identify and diagnose issues before they affect users, ensuring that applications operate efficiently and effectively under varying load conditions. This chapter explores the essential aspects of performance monitoring and analysis using JMeter and Locust, highlighting strategies for collecting, interpreting, and acting on performance data.

Key Performance Metrics

Response Time:

The time it takes for a server to respond to a request from a client. Response time is critical because it directly impacts user experience. Long response times can lead to user frustration and increased bounce rates.

Throughput:

The number of requests processed by the server over a specific period, typically measured in requests per second (RPS). Throughput indicates the server's capacity to handle incoming traffic and is essential for understanding performance under load.

Error Rate:

The percentage of requests that result in errors, such as 4xx or 5xx status codes. A high error rate can signal potential problems in the application or server configuration that need immediate attention.

Concurrent Users:

The number of users simultaneously accessing the application. Understanding how the system performs with varying numbers of concurrent users helps in capacity planning and load testing.

Resource Utilization:

Metrics that indicate how much of the server's resources (CPU, memory, disk I/O, and network bandwidth) are being used during operation. Monitoring resource utilization helps identify bottlenecks and optimize resource allocation.

Latency:

The delay between sending a request and receiving a response. Latency can be caused by various factors, including network delays, server processing time, and client-side rendering.

Saturation:

Refers to the degree to which the system's resources are being utilized. When resources are saturated, it indicates that the system is nearing its capacity limits, which can lead to degraded performance.

User Satisfaction Metrics:

Metrics like the Net Promoter Score (NPS) and Customer Satisfaction Score (CSAT) provide insights into user satisfaction and perceptions of performance. These qualitative metrics can complement quantitative performance data.

Tools for Performance Monitoring

JMeter:

JMeter is primarily used for performance testing but can also be configured for monitoring. Its built-in listeners (e.g., View Results Tree, Summary Report, Response Times Over Time) allow users to visualize performance metrics in real-time during test execution.

JMeter can be integrated with external monitoring tools to capture server-side metrics, providing a comprehensive view of application performance.

Locust:

Locust provides a web-based interface for real-time monitoring of performance metrics during load tests. Users can track response times, request counts, and user behavior dynamically as the test runs.

Locust also allows for custom metrics to be logged and monitored, enabling tailored performance insights based on specific use cases.

Prometheus:

Prometheus is a powerful open-source monitoring and alerting toolkit that is ideal for recording real-time metrics. It is particularly useful for monitoring microservices architectures and can scrape metrics from various sources, including application servers and databases.

Grafana:

Grafana is a visualization tool that integrates with Prometheus and other data sources to create dynamic dashboards. It enables users to visualize performance metrics through graphs and charts, facilitating easy analysis and identification of trends.

New Relic and Datadog:

These are comprehensive application performance monitoring (APM) solutions that provide detailed insights into application performance, user interactions, and resource utilization. They offer real-time monitoring, alerting, and analytics capabilities.

ELK Stack (Elasticsearch, Logstash, Kibana):

The ELK stack is a powerful suite for searching, analyzing, and visualizing log data in real time. It can be utilized to aggregate logs from various services and visualize performance trends and anomalies.

Strategies for Effective Performance Monitoring

Establish Monitoring Goals:

Define clear objectives for what performance metrics are important to monitor based on user expectations, business requirements, and technical constraints. Establish KPIs to track progress toward these goals.

Implement Comprehensive Monitoring:

Ensure that monitoring covers both server-side and client-side metrics. This holistic approach provides a complete picture of performance and user experience, allowing for more effective issue diagnosis.

Set Up Alerts:

Configure alerting mechanisms to notify relevant stakeholders when performance metrics exceed predefined thresholds. Alerts should focus on critical metrics such as response time spikes, error rates, and resource saturation.

Use Real-User Monitoring (RUM):

Implement RUM to gather performance data directly from users' browsers. This data provides insights into how real users experience application performance across different devices and networks.

Analyze Historical Data:

Regularly analyze historical performance data to identify trends and patterns. Understanding how performance evolves over time can inform optimization efforts and capacity planning.

Conduct Root Cause Analysis (RCA):

When performance issues arise, conduct thorough root cause analysis to identify underlying factors contributing to degraded performance. This process should involve collaboration among development, operations, and quality assurance teams.

Integrate Performance Monitoring into CI/CD Pipelines:

Incorporate performance monitoring into continuous integration and continuous deployment (CI/CD) pipelines to catch performance regressions early in the development cycle. Automated tests can validate performance benchmarks before deployment.

Optimize Based on User Feedback:

Leverage user feedback and performance data to drive optimization efforts. Conduct surveys, usability tests, and interviews to gather qualitative insights that complement quantitative performance metrics.

Analyzing Performance Data

Identifying Trends and Patterns:

Regularly analyze performance data to identify trends over time. Look for patterns related to peak usage times, which can inform scaling strategies and load balancing efforts.

Comparative Analysis:

Conduct comparative analyses between different versions of the application or between environments (e.g., staging vs. production). Understanding how performance changes between releases helps identify regression issues.

Correlation Analysis:

Explore correlations between different metrics to uncover relationships between application behavior and performance. For example, analyze how increasing concurrent users affects response times and error rates.

Anomaly Detection:

Utilize machine learning algorithms or statistical methods to detect anomalies in performance data. Identifying deviations from expected behavior can help preemptively address potential performance issues.

User Behavior Analysis:

Analyze how user behavior affects performance metrics. Understanding which features are most frequently used and how users interact with the application can guide optimization priorities.

Feedback Loop:

Create a feedback loop where performance data informs development decisions. Regularly communicate insights gained from performance analysis to development teams to drive continuous improvement.

Best Practices for Performance Monitoring and Analysis

Define Clear Metrics:

Clearly define the metrics you intend to monitor and ensure that they align with business objectives and user expectations. This focus will guide your monitoring efforts.

Regularly Review Performance:

Schedule regular reviews of performance metrics with relevant stakeholders to ensure alignment and prompt action on emerging issues.

Educate Teams on Performance Metrics:

Provide training to development and operations teams on interpreting performance metrics and understanding their implications. This knowledge fosters a culture of performance awareness.

Document Monitoring Processes:

Maintain detailed documentation of monitoring processes, including configurations, tools used, and analysis methodologies. This documentation serves as a valuable resource for new team members and for continuous improvement.

Continuously Evolve Monitoring Strategies:

As applications and user expectations evolve, so should your monitoring strategies. Regularly assess the effectiveness of your monitoring approach and make adjustments as necessary.

Effective performance monitoring and analysis are essential components of successful application management. By establishing robust monitoring practices and leveraging tools like JMeter, Locust, and APM solutions, organizations can gain valuable insights into application performance, identify bottlenecks, and implement optimizations that enhance user experience. Continuous monitoring and analysis will empower teams to maintain high-performance standards, ensuring that applications remain responsive and reliable in a competitive landscape.

Chapter 11: Load Testing Best Practices with JMeter and Locust

Introduction to Load Testing

Load testing is a critical aspect of performance testing that focuses on assessing how an application behaves under expected and peak load conditions. The goal is to identify performance bottlenecks and ensure that the system can handle the anticipated user traffic without degradation in performance. This chapter outlines best practices for load testing using JMeter and Locust, emphasizing the importance of thorough planning, execution, and analysis to achieve meaningful results.

Planning Your Load Testing

Define Objectives and Goals:

Clearly outline the objectives of the load test. Determine what specific metrics you want to evaluate, such as response times, throughput, error rates, and resource utilization.

Set realistic goals based on expected user traffic and performance requirements. These goals should align with business objectives and user expectations.

Understand User Behavior:

Analyze user behavior to create realistic load scenarios. Understand how users interact with the application, including common workflows and peak usage times.

Conduct surveys, user interviews, or analytics reviews to gather insights on user patterns that should be reflected in load tests.

Identify Key Scenarios:

Determine which scenarios are critical for your application's success. Focus on high-traffic workflows, such as user logins, searches, or transaction processing.

Create user journey maps to visualize how different user paths impact performance. Prioritize testing scenarios that are most representative of actual user behavior.

Establish Success Criteria:

Define what constitutes success for the load test. This may include acceptable response times, maximum allowable error rates, or minimum throughput levels.

Involve stakeholders in defining these criteria to ensure alignment with business goals and user satisfaction expectations.

Prepare the Test Environment:

Set up a testing environment that closely resembles the production environment. This includes hardware specifications, software configurations, and network conditions.

Ensure that the test environment is isolated from production to prevent interference with live operations.

Designing Load Test Scenarios

Create User Profiles:

Develop user profiles that represent different segments of your user base. Each profile should have distinct behaviors and usage patterns, such as heavy users, casual users, and administrative users.

Use these profiles to simulate diverse load conditions during testing, ensuring that your tests reflect the varying demands on the application.

Implement Parameterization:

Use parameterization to simulate realistic user interactions by varying input data. For example, use different usernames, passwords, or search queries in each virtual user to mimic real-world usage.

Parameterization helps to avoid caching effects and provides more accurate results.

Incorporate Think Times:

Introduce think times between requests to simulate real user behavior. Users do not execute actions instantaneously; they typically pause to read content or make decisions.

Incorporating think times helps create a more realistic load scenario and reduces the likelihood of overloading the application.

Set Up Ramp-Up Periods:

Configure ramp-up periods to gradually increase the load over time rather than starting with the maximum number of users immediately. This approach helps identify how the system handles incremental load increases.

A typical ramp-up period might range from a few minutes to an hour, depending on the expected load and system capabilities.

Executing Load Tests

Use Distributed Testing:

For large-scale load tests, consider using distributed testing architectures where multiple machines generate load simultaneously. JMeter and Locust both support distributed testing, enabling you to scale your tests effectively.

Distributed testing can simulate thousands or even millions of virtual users, providing a more comprehensive evaluation of system performance.

Monitor Performance During Testing:

Continuously monitor system performance during load tests using tools like JMeter's listeners, Locust's web interface, or external monitoring solutions.

Track key performance metrics in real time, including response times, throughput, and resource utilization, to identify potential bottlenecks as they occur.

Capture Detailed Logs:

Enable detailed logging during load tests to capture all request and response data. This information can be invaluable for diagnosing issues and understanding system behavior under load.

Ensure logs include timestamps, status codes, and any error messages to facilitate analysis.

Test in Iterative Cycles:

Conduct load tests in iterative cycles, making adjustments based on results and insights gained. After each test, analyze performance data and refine test scenarios as necessary.

Iterative testing allows teams to systematically identify and address performance issues.

Analyzing Load Test Results

Review Performance Metrics:

Analyze the collected performance metrics against the established success criteria. Focus on key metrics such as response times, throughput, error rates, and resource utilization.

Look for patterns or anomalies in the data that may indicate performance bottlenecks or areas for improvement.

Identify Bottlenecks:

Use the results to identify specific bottlenecks in the application. Common areas to investigate include slow database queries, inefficient code paths, or resource contention.

Conduct root cause analysis to determine the underlying causes of performance issues.

Generate Detailed Reports:

Create comprehensive reports summarizing the load test findings, including performance metrics, identified bottlenecks, and recommendations for optimization.

Share these reports with stakeholders to facilitate informed decision-making regarding application performance.

Conduct Post-Test Reviews:

Organize post-test reviews with relevant teams to discuss results, insights, and action items. Collaborative discussions help ensure that everyone is aligned on the next steps for optimization.

Use feedback from team members to refine future load testing processes.

Best Practices for Load Testing

Involve Stakeholders:

Engage relevant stakeholders throughout the load testing process, from planning to execution and analysis. Their input can provide valuable insights into business priorities and performance expectations.

Use Version Control for Test Plans:

Maintain version control for load test plans and scripts. This practice allows teams to track changes over time and revert to previous versions if necessary.

Regularly Update Load Test Scenarios:

Keep load test scenarios up to date with changes to the application and user behavior. Regular updates ensure that tests remain relevant and accurately reflect real-world usage.

Automate Load Testing Processes:

Consider automating load testing as part of your continuous integration and deployment (CI/CD) pipeline. Automated load tests can run alongside functional tests, providing timely feedback on performance with each code change.

Benchmark Regularly:

Establish benchmarks for key performance metrics and regularly test against these benchmarks to track performance trends over time. Regular benchmarking can help identify regressions and maintain optimal performance.

Document Learnings:

Keep detailed records of load test outcomes, methodologies, and lessons learned. This documentation serves as a resource for future load testing efforts and can help onboard new team members.

Prioritize User Experience:

Always keep user experience in mind during load testing. Ensure that performance metrics align with user expectations and prioritize optimizations that enhance user satisfaction.

Test Beyond Peak Loads:

While peak load testing is crucial, also consider testing for sustained loads and scenarios beyond expected peak usage. This approach helps identify how the application performs over extended periods under high traffic.

Load testing is an essential practice for ensuring that web applications and APIs can handle expected traffic without performance degradation. By following the best practices outlined in this chapter, teams can design effective load testing strategies using JMeter and Locust that yield valuable insights into system behavior under load. Thorough planning, execution, and analysis will empower organizations to optimize performance, enhance user satisfaction, and maintain a competitive edge in the digital landscape.

Chapter 12: Integrating JMeter and Locust in CI/CD Pipelines

Introduction to CI/CD

Continuous Integration (CI) and Continuous Deployment (CD) are software development practices that aim to automate and improve the processes of integrating code changes and deploying applications. CI/CD allows development teams to deliver high-quality software rapidly and reliably. Integrating performance testing tools like JMeter and Locust into CI/CD pipelines is essential for ensuring that applications not only function correctly but also meet performance requirements throughout the development lifecycle. This chapter explores the best practices for integrating JMeter and Locust into CI/CD pipelines to enhance performance testing.

Understanding the CI/CD Pipeline

Continuous Integration:

CI involves automatically building and testing code every time a team member commits changes to version control. This practice allows teams to detect and fix issues early, improving code quality and collaboration.

Automated tests, including performance tests, are executed as part of the CI process to ensure that new code does not introduce regressions.

Continuous Deployment:

CD extends CI by automating the deployment of applications to production environments after passing automated tests. This practice enables teams to release software updates more frequently and with greater confidence.

Performance tests play a critical role in CD by validating that the application meets performance benchmarks before deployment.

Why Integrate Performance Testing in CI/CD

Early Detection of Performance Issues:

Integrating performance testing into CI/CD allows teams to identify performance bottlenecks early in the development process. Early detection reduces the risk of costly fixes later in the lifecycle.

Consistent Performance Validation:

Automated performance tests ensure that every code change is validated against predefined performance benchmarks. This consistency helps maintain high-performance standards across iterations.

Faster Feedback Loops:

Automated performance testing provides immediate feedback to developers, allowing them to address performance issues as they arise. Faster feedback loops enhance collaboration and promote a culture of performance awareness.

Improved Release Confidence:

By incorporating performance tests into the CI/CD pipeline, teams can deploy updates with confidence, knowing that the application meets both functional and performance criteria.

Preparing Your Environment

Choose the Right CI/CD Tools:

Select CI/CD tools that support integration with performance testing tools. Popular CI/CD platforms like Jenkins, GitLab CI, CircleCI, and Travis CI can easily integrate with JMeter and Locust.

Set Up Performance Testing Frameworks:

Install and configure JMeter and Locust in the CI/CD environment. Ensure that all necessary dependencies, libraries, and test scripts are available for execution during the CI/CD process.

Version Control:

Store JMeter test plans and Locust scripts in version control systems like Git. This practice ensures that performance tests are versioned alongside application code and can be tracked over time.

Create a Dedicated Testing Environment:

Establish a dedicated environment for performance testing within the CI/CD pipeline. This environment should closely mirror the production setup to provide accurate results.

Integrating JMeter into CI/CD Pipelines

Setting Up JMeter in CI/CD:

Use plugins or scripts to execute JMeter tests as part of the CI/CD pipeline. For example, in Jenkins, the JMeter Performance Plugin can be used to run tests and visualize results.

Create a build step in the pipeline to execute JMeter tests, specifying the location of JMeter test plans and any necessary parameters.

Parameterizing JMeter Tests:

Parameterize JMeter test plans to enable dynamic input of variables during execution. This approach allows for flexibility in testing different scenarios without modifying the test plan.

Reporting Results:

Configure JMeter to generate detailed reports after test execution. Use the JMeter HTML Report Dashboard or integrate with external reporting tools for better visualization and analysis.

Store performance test results as artifacts in the CI/CD pipeline, allowing stakeholders to review and analyze them.

Failing the Build on Performance Issues:

Define performance thresholds that, when exceeded, will trigger a failure in the CI/CD pipeline. This practice ensures that only applications meeting performance criteria are deployed to production.

Running JMeter Tests in Parallel:

Optimize performance testing by running JMeter tests in parallel across multiple nodes. This approach simulates higher user loads and provides a more comprehensive evaluation of application performance.

Integrating Locust into CI/CD Pipelines

Setting Up Locust in CI/CD:

Install Locust and set up the necessary configurations in your CI/CD environment. Locust can be easily executed using command-line interfaces, making it suitable for integration into CI/CD pipelines.

Use Docker containers for Locust if your CI/CD environment supports containerization. This setup simplifies dependencies and environment management.

Parameterizing Locust Tests:

Similar to JMeter, parameterize Locust scripts to allow for dynamic user behavior and varying input data during execution. This capability enhances the realism of load tests.

Monitoring Locust Tests:

Use Locust's web interface to monitor performance in real-time. While this is not always feasible in a CI/CD context, capturing and storing metrics in a log file for analysis is a good practice.

Generating Reports:

Implement mechanisms to generate reports after Locust tests. Although Locust does not have built-in reporting like JMeter, you can export metrics in CSV or JSON format and use external tools for visualization.

Failing the Build on Performance Criteria:

Set performance thresholds for Locust tests to ensure builds fail if the application does not meet performance criteria. This practice aligns with the goal of delivering high-quality software.

Best Practices for CI/CD Performance Testing

Start Small and Scale:

Begin with smaller, targeted performance tests in the CI/CD pipeline. As your confidence in the testing process grows, scale up to more comprehensive tests.

Run Tests on Every Commit:

Configure performance tests to run on every commit or pull request. This approach ensures that performance regressions are caught early in the development cycle.

Incorporate Performance Testing into User Acceptance Testing (UAT):

Integrate performance testing as part of the UAT process to validate both functional and performance requirements before production deployment.

Regularly Review Performance Tests:

Periodically review and update performance test plans and scripts to ensure they remain relevant as the application evolves. This practice helps maintain the effectiveness of performance testing efforts.

Foster a Performance-Centric Culture:

Encourage collaboration between development, operations, and QA teams to foster a culture of performance awareness. Performance should be a shared responsibility across the organization.

Use Feedback for Continuous Improvement:

Analyze performance test results and gather feedback from team members to improve testing strategies and methodologies continually. This process fosters a cycle of continuous improvement.

Document Testing Processes:

Maintain thorough documentation of the performance testing processes, configurations, and results. This documentation serves as a valuable resource for training new team members and improving future efforts.

Integrating performance testing tools like JMeter and Locust into CI/CD pipelines is essential for maintaining high-performance standards in modern software development. By following best practices for integration, organizations can ensure that performance is a key consideration throughout the development lifecycle. This proactive approach to performance testing not only enhances application quality but also contributes to user satisfaction and business success.

Chapter 13: Advanced Load Testing Techniques with JMeter and Locust

Introduction to Advanced Load Testing Techniques

As web applications and services continue to evolve in complexity and scale, the need for advanced load testing techniques becomes increasingly important. Standard load testing methods may not fully capture the intricacies of modern applications, necessitating more sophisticated approaches to ensure optimal performance under various conditions. This chapter delves into advanced load testing techniques using JMeter and Locust, exploring methods such as distributed testing, real-time monitoring, cloud-based load generation, and incorporating artificial intelligence (AI) and machine learning (ML) into load testing strategies.

Distributed Load Testing

Understanding Distributed Load Testing:

Distributed load testing involves spreading the load generation across multiple machines or nodes to simulate a large number of users. This approach is essential for testing applications that need to handle significant traffic volumes.

Both JMeter and Locust support distributed load testing, enabling users to scale their tests effectively.

Setting Up Distributed Testing with JMeter:

Configuration of JMeter Slave Instances: To configure JMeter for distributed testing, set up one master instance (the controller) and multiple slave instances (load generators). Each slave will run a copy of the test plan, generating requests to the target server.

Running Tests in Distributed Mode: Use the command line or the JMeter GUI to start the master and slave instances. The master sends the test plan to the slaves, coordinates the execution, and collects the results.

Monitoring Distributed Tests: Use JMeter's built-in listeners or external monitoring tools to track performance metrics during distributed tests, ensuring that data from all slave instances is aggregated for analysis.

Setting Up Distributed Testing with Locust:

Locust Swarm Mode: Locust natively supports distributed load generation through its swarm mode. Start a master node to manage the test and multiple worker nodes to generate load.

Deploying Workers in Different Locations: For realistic testing, deploy worker nodes in various geographic locations to simulate users from different regions. This approach allows for testing latency and performance across different environments.

Real-Time Monitoring with Locust: Utilize Locust's web interface to monitor performance in real-time during distributed testing, visualizing metrics such as request rates, response times, and error rates.

Cloud-Based Load Testing

Advantages of Cloud-Based Load Testing:

Cloud-based load testing provides flexibility, scalability, and cost-effectiveness. Organizations can leverage cloud resources to generate load without the need for extensive on-premises infrastructure.

The ability to quickly provision and deprovision resources allows for efficient management of load testing environments.

Using JMeter in the Cloud:

JMeter on Cloud Providers: Deploy JMeter instances on cloud platforms like AWS, Azure, or Google Cloud. Use instances to run JMeter tests, leveraging cloud scalability to generate high loads.

Integration with Cloud Load Testing Services: Several cloud load testing services, such as BlazeMeter, offer integration with JMeter. These platforms allow users to upload JMeter test plans and execute tests in the cloud, providing comprehensive reporting and analysis tools.

Using Locust in the Cloud:

Deploying Locust on Cloud Instances: Similar to JMeter, Locust can be deployed on cloud instances. Use cloud virtual machines to run Locust tests and simulate user traffic efficiently.

Cloud-Based Load Testing Services: Utilize cloud-based services that support Locust, allowing for easy setup and execution of load tests. These services provide dashboards for monitoring performance metrics and visualizing results.

Real-Time Monitoring and Analysis

Importance of Real-Time Monitoring:

Real-time monitoring during load tests is crucial for identifying performance bottlenecks as they occur. Immediate feedback enables teams to address issues promptly and adjust testing parameters if needed.

By monitoring key performance metrics such as CPU utilization, memory usage, and network latency, teams can gain insights into system behavior under load.

Real-Time Monitoring with JMeter:

Using Listeners for Real-Time Feedback: JMeter includes several listeners, such as Aggregate Report and Summary Report, that can display performance metrics in real-time during test execution.

Integrating with Monitoring Tools: Integrate JMeter with external monitoring tools like Grafana, Prometheus, or New Relic to visualize performance metrics in real-time dashboards. This integration allows for comprehensive analysis and troubleshooting during load tests.

Real-Time Monitoring with Locust:

Locust Web Interface: Locust provides a built-in web interface that displays real-time statistics on active users, request rates, response times, and failures. This interface allows teams to monitor performance as tests progress.

Custom Metrics and Logging: Customize Locust to log additional metrics or events during tests. Use this data for deeper analysis and correlation with application performance.

Incorporating AI and Machine Learning in Load Testing

The Role of AI and ML in Load Testing:

AI and machine learning can enhance load testing strategies by analyzing historical performance data and predicting system behavior under various load conditions. These technologies enable teams to identify patterns and optimize testing efforts.

By leveraging AI and ML algorithms, organizations can improve the accuracy and effectiveness of load tests, ultimately leading to better performance outcomes.

Predictive Analysis for Load Testing:

Using Historical Data: Collect historical performance data from previous load tests and use machine learning algorithms to analyze trends and predict how the application will perform under future loads.

Dynamic Load Adjustment: Implement algorithms that can dynamically adjust load generation based on real-time system performance. If the system starts to exhibit signs of strain, the load can be reduced or modified accordingly.

Automating Test Generation:

AI-Driven Test Creation: Utilize AI tools to analyze application usage patterns and automatically generate load test scripts. This approach reduces the time required for test creation and ensures that tests are relevant and reflective of real-world usage.

Continuous Learning: Implement a system where load testing frameworks continuously learn from past tests and adjust parameters or scenarios to improve accuracy and relevance.

Using Protocols and Load Testing Patterns

Testing with Different Protocols:

HTTP/HTTPS Testing: Standard web applications primarily use the HTTP/HTTPS protocol. Ensure that load tests cover various HTTP methods, including GET, POST, PUT, and DELETE.

WebSocket and Streaming Protocols: Many modern applications rely on WebSocket or other streaming protocols. JMeter and Locust can be configured to test these protocols, ensuring that real-time features perform well under load.

Adopting Load Testing Patterns:

Step Load Testing: Gradually increase the load in predefined steps, allowing teams to observe performance at various levels. This approach helps identify the point at which the application begins to experience degradation.

Spike Testing: Simulate sudden spikes in traffic to evaluate how the system responds to unexpected loads. Spike testing is useful for understanding application resilience and recovery capabilities.

Soak Testing: Conduct long-duration tests to assess how the application performs under sustained load over time. Soak testing helps identify issues related to resource leaks or degradation over time.

Chaos Engineering in Load Testing:

Introducing Controlled Failures: Incorporate chaos engineering principles into load testing by introducing controlled failures (e.g., shutting down services, simulating network latency) to observe how the system reacts.

Enhancing Resilience Testing: By subjecting applications to real-world failure scenarios during load tests, teams can better understand application resilience and improve recovery strategies.

Advanced load testing techniques are essential for modern applications, ensuring they can withstand the pressures of high user traffic and complex usage patterns. By leveraging distributed load testing, cloud-based solutions, real-time monitoring, and integrating AI and ML into load testing strategies, organizations can achieve a deeper understanding of application performance. The methods discussed in this chapter empower teams to design more effective load tests that accurately reflect real-world conditions, ultimately leading to better user experiences and application reliability.

Chapter 14: Performance Testing Best Practices with JMeter and Locust

Introduction to Performance Testing Best Practices

Performance testing is a critical component of software development that ensures applications can handle expected user loads while meeting performance criteria. JMeter and Locust are two powerful tools for conducting performance tests, but the effectiveness of these tools depends significantly on the best practices implemented during testing. This chapter outlines key best practices for performance testing with JMeter and Locust, focusing on test planning, execution, analysis, and maintenance.

Test Planning

Define Clear Objectives:

Before initiating performance testing, establish clear and measurable objectives. Understand what aspects of performance are being tested, such as response times, throughput, or resource utilization.

Identify the key performance indicators (KPIs) relevant to your application. Common KPIs include average response time, maximum response time, error rate, and resource utilization (CPU, memory, disk I/O).

Understand User Behavior:

Analyze user behavior to create realistic load scenarios. Understand how users interact with the application, including typical user journeys, peak usage times, and variations in usage patterns.

Create user personas and scenarios that reflect actual user behavior. This practice helps ensure that load tests mimic real-world usage, providing more relevant results.

Determine Load Testing Types:

Identify the types of performance tests to be conducted, such as load testing, stress testing, spike testing, endurance testing, and scalability testing. Each type serves a different purpose and should be tailored to meet specific objectives.

Consider conducting baseline tests to establish a performance baseline before adding complexity. This approach helps identify performance degradation due to code changes or new features.

Choose Appropriate Test Data:

Prepare realistic and diverse test data that mirrors production data. This practice ensures that tests are comprehensive and yield meaningful results.

Consider using data generation tools to create dynamic data sets for testing. This approach prevents the use of static data, which may not accurately reflect real-world scenarios.

Test Execution

Use Realistic Load Models:

Design load models that replicate expected traffic patterns. This includes defining the number of users, ramp-up periods, and steady-state durations.

Ensure that tests simulate different user load patterns, such as normal load, peak load, and sudden spikes. This approach helps identify performance issues that may arise under various conditions.

Implement Distributed Load Testing:

For applications expecting high user traffic, consider using distributed load testing techniques with JMeter and Locust. Distributing load generation across multiple machines allows for realistic simulation of large-scale user interactions.

Ensure that the testing environment mirrors the production environment to provide accurate results.

Monitor System Performance:

Utilize monitoring tools to track system performance metrics during load tests. Metrics to monitor include CPU usage, memory consumption, disk I/O, network latency, and application-specific performance metrics.

JMeter and Locust allow integration with monitoring tools such as Grafana or New Relic to visualize metrics in real-time, providing insights into system behavior under load.

Gradually Increase Load:

Implement a gradual ramp-up of users during testing. This approach helps to identify the system's breaking point and allows for more accurate observations of performance characteristics.

Monitor system responses as the load increases, looking for signs of degradation, such as increased response times or error rates.

Test Analysis

Analyze Test Results Thoroughly:

After executing performance tests, analyze the results to identify trends, bottlenecks, and areas for improvement. Focus on both high-level metrics and detailed logs to gain comprehensive insights.

Utilize built-in reporting features in JMeter and Locust to generate visual reports. These reports can help communicate findings effectively to stakeholders.

Correlate Data with Performance Metrics:

Establish correlations between different performance metrics. For instance, examine how increased user load correlates with changes in response times or resource utilization.

Identify outliers and anomalies in the data. Understanding these anomalies can provide insights into underlying issues affecting performance.

Document Findings:

Maintain detailed documentation of test results, analysis, and observations. This documentation serves as a valuable resource for future testing efforts and helps track improvements over time.

Include recommendations for performance enhancements based on the analysis. This practice fosters continuous improvement in application performance.

Test Maintenance

Regularly Update Performance Tests:

As the application evolves, regularly update performance test scripts to reflect changes in functionality, user behavior, and application architecture.

Conduct periodic reviews of existing tests to ensure they remain relevant and effective. Remove outdated tests and add new scenarios as necessary.

Automate Performance Testing:

Integrate performance testing into CI/CD pipelines to automate execution and ensure that tests run consistently with every code change. Automation enhances testing efficiency and reduces manual effort.

Use tools like Jenkins or GitLab CI to schedule regular performance tests, capturing metrics over time to identify trends and improvements.

Perform Retrospective Analyses:

After each testing cycle, conduct retrospective analyses to evaluate the effectiveness of the performance testing strategy. Identify lessons learned and areas for improvement.

Engage all stakeholders in the retrospective process to gather diverse perspectives and insights that can enhance future testing efforts.

Establish a Culture of Performance:

Foster a culture of performance awareness within the development team. Encourage developers to consider performance implications during the coding phase, leading to better design choices and coding practices.

Provide training and resources to team members to enhance their understanding of performance testing best practices. This knowledge will empower them to contribute effectively to performance testing efforts.

Implementing best practices for performance testing with JMeter and Locust is essential for achieving reliable and meaningful results. By focusing on comprehensive test planning, realistic execution, thorough analysis, and diligent maintenance, organizations can ensure their applications are optimized for performance under real-world conditions. Adopting these best practices fosters a proactive approach to performance testing, ultimately leading to enhanced user satisfaction and application reliability.

Chapter 15: Troubleshooting Performance Issues with JMeter and Locust

Introduction to Troubleshooting Performance Issues

Troubleshooting performance issues is a critical aspect of performance testing and optimization. Regardless of the tools employed, such as JMeter and Locust, performance issues can arise from various sources, including application code, server configurations, network infrastructure, or external dependencies. This chapter provides a comprehensive approach to troubleshooting performance issues, focusing on the identification, diagnosis, and resolution of common problems encountered during load testing.

Identifying Performance Bottlenecks

Establish Baseline Performance Metrics:

Before troubleshooting, it's essential to have a clear understanding of baseline performance metrics. These metrics serve as a reference point for identifying deviations during load testing.

Key performance indicators (KPIs) to establish include response times, throughput, error rates, and resource utilization metrics such as CPU, memory, and disk I/O.

Monitor Performance During Load Testing:

Utilize built-in monitoring features in JMeter and Locust to track performance metrics in real time during load tests. Monitoring tools can provide insights into system behavior and help identify bottlenecks as they occur.

Collect data on various performance metrics, including average and maximum response times, server response codes, and resource usage. This information is crucial for pinpointing performance issues.

Analyze Response Times:

Break down response times into key components, such as connection time, server processing time, and response retrieval time. This granularity helps identify where delays occur in the request-response cycle.

Use JMeter's Listener components (such as the Response Time Graph) or Locust's real-time web interface to visualize response time distributions and identify spikes or anomalies.

Check Error Rates:

Monitor error rates during load tests to identify potential issues with the application. High error rates can indicate underlying problems, such as incorrect configurations, application bugs, or resource limitations.

Analyze error logs to understand the root causes of failures. In JMeter, the "View Results Tree" listener provides detailed information about failed requests, including response codes and messages.

Diagnosing Performance Issues

Examine System Resource Utilization:

Analyze CPU, memory, disk, and network utilization during load tests. High resource utilization can lead to performance degradation and should be monitored closely.

Use system monitoring tools such as top, htop, or resource monitors in cloud environments to assess how resources are being consumed during the load test.

Evaluate Application Logs:

Review application logs for error messages, warnings, or exceptions that occur during the test. Logs often provide valuable insights into application behavior and can highlight issues affecting performance.

Look for patterns in log entries that coincide with performance degradation. For example, a spike in error logs may correlate with increased load.

Analyze Database Performance:

Database performance can significantly impact application performance. Analyze database query performance, including execution times, lock contention, and resource usage.

Use database profiling tools to identify slow queries and optimize them. JMeter can also be configured to simulate database load to assess performance under realistic conditions.

Network Analysis:

Evaluate network performance to identify potential bottlenecks. High latency or packet loss can lead to increased response times and reduced application performance.

Utilize network monitoring tools to assess bandwidth usage, latency, and connectivity issues. Tools like Wireshark can help capture and analyze network traffic.

Resolving Performance Issues

Optimize Application Code:

Once bottlenecks are identified, collaborate with development teams to optimize application code. Focus on reducing processing times, optimizing algorithms, and improving code efficiency.

Implement best practices such as caching frequently accessed data, reducing database calls, and optimizing resource-heavy operations.

Adjust Server Configuration:

Review and adjust server configurations based on performance test results. This may include tuning application servers, web servers, and database servers for optimal performance.

Adjust parameters such as connection pool sizes, thread limits, and timeout settings to better handle the expected load.

Scaling Infrastructure:

If performance issues are related to resource limitations, consider scaling the infrastructure. This can involve vertical scaling (upgrading existing hardware) or horizontal scaling (adding more servers).

Utilize cloud-based solutions for on-demand scalability, allowing for quick adjustments to resources based on testing requirements.

Implement Load Balancing:

If applicable, implement load balancing strategies to distribute traffic evenly across servers. This approach helps prevent any single server from becoming a performance bottleneck.

Configure load balancers to monitor server health and route traffic intelligently, ensuring high availability and optimal performance.

Conduct Regression Testing:

After resolving performance issues, conduct regression testing to ensure that changes made do not introduce new problems or regress performance.

Rerun performance tests under similar conditions to validate that the identified issues have been resolved and that the application meets performance expectations.

Continuous Performance Monitoring

Establish Continuous Monitoring Practices:

Implement continuous performance monitoring practices to identify issues proactively. This approach allows for the detection of performance degradation before it impacts users.

Use application performance monitoring (APM) tools to monitor application performance in real-time. Tools like New Relic, AppDynamics, or Dynatrace can provide insights into performance metrics, transaction traces, and bottlenecks.

Integrate Performance Testing into CI/CD Pipelines:

Integrate performance testing into the continuous integration and continuous deployment (CI/CD) pipeline to ensure that performance is evaluated with every code change.

Automated performance tests can be scheduled to run during builds or deployments, providing quick feedback on performance impacts.

Regularly Review Performance Metrics:

Conduct regular reviews of performance metrics to identify trends and anomalies over time. Historical data can provide valuable insights into application performance and user behavior.

Set up alerts for performance thresholds, enabling teams to respond quickly to emerging issues.

Best Practices for Performance Troubleshooting

Document Performance Issues and Resolutions:

Maintain thorough documentation of performance issues encountered during testing, including their resolutions and any changes made. This documentation serves as a valuable reference for future troubleshooting efforts.

Create a knowledge base that includes common issues, resolutions, and best practices to guide future performance testing initiatives.

Collaborate Across Teams:

Foster collaboration between development, QA, and operations teams to address performance issues effectively. Sharing insights and expertise can lead to more efficient troubleshooting and problem resolution.

Encourage cross-functional teams to participate in performance testing efforts, promoting a culture of performance awareness throughout the organization.

Adopt a Proactive Approach:

Adopt a proactive approach to performance testing and troubleshooting. Anticipate potential performance issues based on application complexity and user demand.

Conduct regular performance audits and assessments to ensure that the application remains optimized for performance over time.

Troubleshooting performance issues with JMeter and Locust requires a systematic approach to identifying, diagnosing, and resolving problems. By establishing baseline metrics, monitoring performance during load tests, analyzing system behavior, and collaborating across teams, organizations can effectively address performance challenges. Implementing continuous performance monitoring and integrating performance testing into CI/CD pipelines further enhances the ability to proactively manage application performance, ensuring optimal user experiences and application reliability.

Chapter 16: Integrating JMeter and Locust with CI/CD Pipelines

Introduction to CI/CD Integration

Continuous Integration and Continuous Deployment (CI/CD) have revolutionized software development, enabling teams to deliver code changes quickly and efficiently. Integrating performance testing tools like JMeter and Locust into CI/CD pipelines ensures that performance considerations are part of the development process, allowing teams to identify and address performance issues early in the software lifecycle. This chapter discusses the best practices for integrating JMeter and Locust into CI/CD workflows, covering configuration, execution, reporting, and continuous improvement.

Understanding CI/CD Fundamentals

Defining Continuous Integration (CI):

Continuous Integration involves automatically building and testing code changes in a shared repository. The goal is to identify integration issues early and improve the quality of software by ensuring that changes do not break existing functionality.

CI typically includes automated unit tests, integration tests, and performance tests. By running performance tests in the CI pipeline, teams can catch performance regressions before they reach production.

Understanding Continuous Deployment (CD):

Continuous Deployment automates the release of code changes to production environments after passing tests. This practice allows teams to deploy new features, bug fixes, and improvements rapidly and reliably.

CD pipelines can also include performance validation steps to ensure that deployments do not degrade application performance.

Importance of Performance Testing in CI/CD:

Integrating performance testing into CI/CD ensures that performance is a continuous concern rather than an afterthought. It helps teams maintain performance standards as they iterate on their applications.

Early detection of performance issues reduces the risk of deploying subpar application versions that could lead to poor user experiences.

Setting Up JMeter and Locust for CI/CD

Preparing JMeter for CI/CD Integration:

To integrate JMeter into a CI/CD pipeline, create JMeter test scripts that can be executed in a non-GUI mode. This mode is ideal for automation and reduces resource consumption during test execution.

Organize JMeter test scripts in a version-controlled repository. Ensure that scripts are easily accessible to the CI/CD pipeline.

Configuring Locust for CI/CD Execution:

Locust is designed to be run from the command line, making it straightforward to integrate into CI/CD pipelines. Define test scenarios and configure Locust to simulate realistic user behavior in your performance tests.

Store Locust test scripts in a version-controlled repository, similar to JMeter scripts, to enable easy access and modification.

Selecting CI/CD Tools:

Choose a CI/CD tool that supports integration with JMeter and Locust. Popular tools include Jenkins, GitLab CI/CD, CircleCI, Travis CI, and GitHub Actions.

Ensure that the chosen CI/CD tool can run shell commands and has the necessary plugins to support JMeter and Locust execution.

Executing Performance Tests in CI/CD

Creating Pipeline Steps for Performance Testing:

Define pipeline steps that trigger performance tests after successful builds or unit tests. This ensures that performance is assessed before deploying to staging or production environments.

For JMeter, use command-line execution with the jmeter command to run test scripts. For example: bash

```
jmeter -n -t test_plan.jmx -l results.jtl
```

For Locust, execute tests with a command like: bash

```
locust -f locustfile.py --headless -u 100 -r 10 --host
http://yourapp.com
```

Environment Configuration:

Configure environment variables to define parameters such as test duration, user load, and target URLs. This configuration allows for flexibility and adaptability in different environments (e.g., staging vs. production).

Ensure that the CI/CD environment has the necessary resources (CPU, memory) to execute performance tests effectively. Consider using dedicated resources for load testing to avoid interference with other pipeline activities.

Running Performance Tests Concurrently:

Implement parallel execution of performance tests where feasible to reduce overall testing time. Both JMeter and Locust support distributed load testing, enabling tests to be executed across multiple machines.

Configure your CI/CD tool to trigger multiple test instances concurrently, simulating a higher user load while keeping resource usage in check.

Reporting and Analyzing Performance Test Results

Generating Test Reports:

Configure JMeter and Locust to generate detailed test reports that include performance metrics, response times, and error rates. JMeter provides built-in listeners that can produce various reports, while Locust can output results in CSV or HTML formats.

Set up the CI/CD pipeline to publish test reports automatically. This practice allows stakeholders to access performance data without manual intervention.

Integrating Performance Metrics into CI/CD Dashboards:

Incorporate performance metrics into CI/CD dashboards using tools like Grafana, Kibana, or the built-in dashboards of CI/CD tools. This integration provides visibility into performance trends and highlights regressions.

Use monitoring tools to capture real-time performance metrics during test execution. Combine these metrics with CI/CD results to provide a holistic view of application performance.

Establishing Thresholds and Alerts:

Define performance thresholds that must be met for each deployment. For example, establish maximum acceptable response times or error rates. If tests exceed these thresholds, the pipeline should fail or send alerts to the development team.

Implement automated notifications via email, Slack, or other messaging services to inform team members of performance test outcomes, especially when thresholds are breached.

Continuous Improvement in Performance Testing

Regularly Review Test Strategies:

Continuously evaluate and refine performance testing strategies based on insights gained from CI/CD executions. Regular reviews help teams adapt to changing application requirements and user behavior.

Encourage feedback loops between development and testing teams to identify areas for improvement in performance testing practices.

Incorporate User Feedback:

Integrate user feedback into performance testing strategies. Conduct performance tests that simulate user scenarios based on actual user interactions, ensuring that testing remains relevant.

Use feedback from production performance monitoring to inform test design and identify scenarios that require additional testing.

Training and Knowledge Sharing:

Provide training sessions for team members on using JMeter and Locust effectively within the CI/CD context. Encourage knowledge sharing to enhance the team's understanding of performance testing best practices.

Create documentation that outlines CI/CD integration processes, test execution commands, and troubleshooting tips. This resource will help new team members onboard quickly and efficiently.

Challenges and Considerations

Handling Flaky Tests:

Address flaky performance tests that may yield inconsistent results. Flakiness can arise from environmental issues, timing problems, or insufficient load simulations. Implement retries or enhance the stability of tests.

Review and refine test scripts to ensure they accurately represent user behavior and are not overly sensitive to minor variations.

Resource Management:

Monitor resource usage during performance testing to avoid resource exhaustion. Ensure that the CI/CD environment has adequate resources for both performance tests and other pipeline activities.

Consider using cloud-based load testing solutions to scale resources dynamically based on testing requirements, especially for large-scale performance tests.

Balancing Performance and Other Tests:

Strike a balance between performance testing and other types of testing (e.g., unit testing, integration testing) in the CI/CD pipeline. While performance is essential, ensure that other tests are not neglected.

Allocate appropriate time slots for performance testing within the pipeline to ensure that tests run efficiently without causing delays in the overall build process.

Integrating JMeter and Locust into CI/CD pipelines is a powerful approach to ensure performance is continuously evaluated throughout the software development lifecycle. By configuring performance tests, executing them in the pipeline, analyzing results, and implementing continuous improvement practices, teams can maintain high performance standards. This proactive approach to performance testing enhances the overall quality of software releases, leading to better user experiences and reduced downtime. As organizations embrace CI/CD, the integration of performance testing will become an integral part of the development process, ultimately fostering a culture of quality and performance excellence.

Chapter 17: Best Practices for Load Testing with JMeter and Locust

Introduction to Load Testing Best Practices

Load testing is a crucial aspect of performance testing, helping organizations ensure that their applications can handle anticipated user traffic without degradation in performance. While tools like JMeter and Locust are powerful in their capabilities, following best practices is essential to maximize their effectiveness and ensure reliable, actionable results. This chapter outlines key best practices for load testing using JMeter and Locust, covering test design, execution, analysis, and continuous improvement.

Designing Effective Load Tests

Define Clear Objectives:

Before creating load tests, establish clear objectives based on the application's requirements and expected user behavior. Objectives may include validating response times under different loads, determining the application's maximum capacity, or identifying bottlenecks.

Clearly defined objectives guide the design of the test scenarios and help ensure that the tests provide valuable insights into application performance.

Create Realistic User Scenarios:

Design load tests that simulate realistic user behavior and patterns. This includes considering user paths, transaction sequences, and interactions with the application.

For instance, if an application typically experiences a surge of users logging in simultaneously at peak hours, replicate this scenario in your tests to understand how the application performs under those conditions.

Utilize Parameterization and Correlation:

Use parameterization to simulate multiple users interacting with the application simultaneously. Parameterization involves replacing hardcoded values in the test scripts with dynamic data, such as usernames, passwords, or session tokens.

Implement correlation to handle dynamic data returned by the server, such as session IDs or tokens needed for subsequent requests. This practice ensures that your load tests accurately represent real-world user interactions.

Set Up Appropriate Load Profiles:

Develop load profiles that reflect different user load conditions, such as normal load, peak load, and stress testing. Varying load profiles help assess how the application responds to different traffic conditions.

For example, design a ramp-up period that gradually increases the number of users to observe how the application handles growing load without crashing.

Determine Key Performance Indicators (KPIs):

Identify the key performance indicators to be measured during load testing, such as response times, throughput, error rates, and resource utilization (CPU, memory, disk, etc.).

These KPIs serve as benchmarks to assess the application's performance against defined expectations and can help identify areas for improvement.

Executing Load Tests Effectively

Choose the Right Environment:

Execute load tests in a dedicated testing environment that closely mirrors the production environment. This similarity ensures that results are relevant and can be reliably extrapolated to the production setting.

Avoid running load tests in the same environment as other testing types (e.g., unit tests) to prevent interference that could skew results.

Monitor System Resources:

Continuously monitor system resources (CPU, memory, network bandwidth, etc.) during load tests to identify any resource bottlenecks that may impact performance.

Use external monitoring tools alongside JMeter and Locust to gain insights into server performance. Tools like Grafana, Prometheus, or New Relic can provide valuable metrics that inform the load testing process.

Utilize Distributed Testing:

Leverage distributed load testing capabilities of JMeter and Locust to simulate a larger number of users than a single machine can handle. This approach allows for more extensive testing scenarios and a better understanding of application performance under high load conditions.

Configure multiple load generators to run tests in parallel, distributing the load across multiple machines. This configuration can help reveal issues that may not be apparent with a smaller user load.

Conduct Test Runs and Iterations:

Execute multiple iterations of load tests to obtain reliable results and mitigate the impact of variability in performance due to factors such as server state or external influences.

Analyze test results after each iteration, refining and adjusting test scenarios as necessary to ensure comprehensive coverage of potential performance issues.

Analyzing Load Test Results

Review and Interpret Performance Metrics:

Collect and analyze performance metrics from load tests to understand application behavior under load. Look for patterns in response times, throughput, and error rates to identify potential bottlenecks or performance issues.

Utilize visualizations such as graphs and charts to present results clearly. JMeter provides various reporting options, including summary reports and graphs, while Locust generates real-time statistics during test execution.

Identify Bottlenecks and Issues:

Investigate any anomalies or spikes in response times or error rates observed during load testing. Delve into the system's resource utilization metrics to pinpoint areas of concern.

Analyze logs generated by the application, server, and database to identify specific errors or issues that correlate with performance degradation. This analysis helps direct subsequent optimization efforts.

Compare Against Baseline Metrics:

Compare the results of load tests against established baseline metrics to assess the application's performance. Establishing baseline performance metrics during earlier development stages helps to contextualize current test results.

Identify performance regressions by comparing results over time. This comparison is critical in ensuring that performance standards are maintained as the application evolves.

Continuous Improvement Practices

Implement Feedback Loops:

Establish feedback loops between performance testing and development teams. Use insights gained from load testing to inform developers of potential issues and areas for improvement.

Regularly review performance test results with stakeholders to ensure that everyone is aware of the application's performance status and any necessary adjustments.

Integrate Performance Testing into CI/CD:

Embed load testing within the CI/CD pipeline to ensure that performance is assessed continuously throughout the development lifecycle. By making performance testing part of the release process, teams can catch regressions early.

Automate performance test execution and reporting to streamline the process and enhance collaboration between development and testing teams.

Regularly Update Test Scenarios:

As the application evolves, regularly review and update load test scenarios to reflect new features, changes in user behavior, or shifts in application architecture. This ongoing maintenance ensures that performance testing remains relevant and valuable.

Involve key stakeholders, including developers and product owners, in reviewing test scenarios to ensure that they accurately represent user interactions and application functionality.

Document Learnings and Best Practices:

Maintain documentation of lessons learned from load testing, including test configurations, scenarios, outcomes, and resolutions to identified performance issues. This documentation serves as a valuable resource for future testing efforts.

Share best practices across teams to foster a culture of continuous improvement and performance awareness within the organization.

Common Pitfalls to Avoid

Ignoring Non-Functional Requirements:

Avoid neglecting non-functional requirements during the load testing process. While functional tests verify features, non-functional tests (including performance tests) are equally important to ensure a seamless user experience.

Incorporate performance criteria into acceptance testing to ensure that all application aspects meet user expectations.

Underestimating User Load:

Be cautious not to underestimate the user load during testing. Inaccurate load predictions can lead to performance tests that fail to replicate real-world conditions.

Use historical data and analytics to estimate user load more accurately. Understand peak usage patterns to simulate realistic testing scenarios.

Focusing Solely on Response Times:

While response times are essential, do not focus solely on them at the expense of other performance metrics. Throughput, error rates, and resource utilization provide a more comprehensive view of application performance.

Consider the end-to-end user experience by assessing how the application performs under varying load conditions and measuring metrics that impact user satisfaction.

Failing to Follow Up on Results:

Avoid the pitfall of running tests and not acting on the results. Performance testing is only valuable if the insights gained are translated into actionable improvements.

Establish a process for addressing performance issues identified during testing, including tracking resolutions and validating improvements in subsequent tests.

Following best practices for load testing with JMeter and Locust is crucial for ensuring that applications can handle expected user traffic while maintaining optimal performance. By designing effective tests, executing them thoughtfully, analyzing results comprehensively, and engaging in continuous improvement, organizations can foster a culture of performance excellence. These practices not only lead to better-performing applications but also enhance user satisfaction and confidence in the software being delivered. As technology continues to evolve, staying informed about best practices in load testing will help teams meet the challenges of modern software development effectively.

Chapter 18: Future Trends in Load Testing with JMeter and Locust

Introduction to Emerging Trends

As technology evolves, so do the methodologies and tools used in software testing, particularly in load testing. With the increasing complexity of applications and the growing emphasis on delivering a seamless user experience, organizations must adapt their load testing strategies to keep pace with these changes. This chapter explores the future trends in load testing with JMeter and Locust, focusing on advancements in technology, the rise of new testing methodologies, and the increasing importance of performance testing in agile development environments.

The Shift to Cloud-Based Load Testing

Understanding Cloud Load Testing:

Cloud load testing allows organizations to simulate user traffic from distributed geographic locations using cloud resources. This approach enables scalability and flexibility, making it easier to conduct extensive load tests without the need for physical infrastructure.

With cloud-based load testing, teams can quickly provision and decommission testing environments, reducing costs and increasing efficiency.

161

Benefits of Cloud Load Testing:

Cloud-based testing tools can simulate thousands of concurrent users, making it easier to assess application performance under heavy load. This capability is crucial for applications with fluctuating user traffic, such as e-commerce sites during holiday seasons.

The use of cloud infrastructure enables teams to test applications under various network conditions, enhancing the realism of load testing scenarios. This realism helps identify potential issues related to latency, bandwidth limitations, and regional variations.

Integration with JMeter and Locust:

Both JMeter and Locust can leverage cloud services to perform load testing. For example, JMeter can be integrated with cloud providers like AWS or Azure to utilize their scalable resources for distributed testing.

Locust's design as a Python-based load testing tool makes it easy to deploy on cloud instances, allowing teams to quickly scale their tests according to demand.

Enhanced Use of Artificial Intelligence and Machine Learning

AI and Machine Learning in Load Testing:

The integration of artificial intelligence (AI) and machine learning (ML) in load testing can significantly enhance the effectiveness of performance testing efforts. These technologies can analyze historical performance data, identify patterns, and predict system behavior under different load conditions.

AI-driven testing tools can automatically generate load testing scenarios based on user behavior analysis, ensuring that tests remain relevant as applications evolve.

Automated Root Cause Analysis:

AI and ML can automate the root cause analysis of performance issues identified during load testing. By analyzing logs, performance metrics, and user interactions, AI-driven tools can pinpoint bottlenecks and recommend solutions.

This capability reduces the time spent on diagnosing issues, enabling faster resolution and ensuring that performance problems are addressed promptly.

Predictive Load Testing:

Predictive load testing uses machine learning algorithms to forecast application performance based on historical data and expected traffic patterns. This approach allows teams to proactively identify potential performance issues before they impact users.

Organizations can adjust their testing strategies based on predictions, optimizing resources and ensuring that the application can handle anticipated user loads.

Increased Focus on Continuous Performance Testing

Continuous Performance Testing in Agile Development:

As organizations adopt agile methodologies, the need for continuous performance testing becomes paramount. Integrating performance testing into the CI/CD pipeline ensures that performance is assessed throughout the development lifecycle, rather than as a separate phase.

Continuous performance testing helps teams detect performance regressions early, enabling quicker remediation and maintaining performance standards.

Shift-Left Testing Practices:

The shift-left testing approach emphasizes early testing in the software development lifecycle. By incorporating performance testing early in the development process, teams can identify performance issues during the coding phase rather than after deployment.

JMeter and Locust can be integrated with CI/CD tools, allowing for automated performance tests to run alongside unit and integration tests, ensuring that performance is continuously monitored.

Incorporation of User Feedback:

Continuous performance testing also involves integrating user feedback into the testing process. Analyzing user interactions and experiences can provide valuable insights into how the application performs in real-world conditions.

Organizations can use feedback from production monitoring tools to inform load testing scenarios, ensuring that tests accurately reflect actual user behavior.

The Rise of Microservices and Serverless Architecture

Load Testing Microservices:

The adoption of microservices architectures presents new challenges for load testing. Each microservice can be independently deployed, scaled, and tested, requiring a more granular approach to performance testing.

Load testing tools like JMeter and Locust must adapt to effectively simulate user interactions across multiple microservices, ensuring that performance testing reflects the complexities of distributed systems.

Serverless Load Testing:

With the rise of serverless computing, load testing strategies must evolve. Serverless architectures automatically scale based on demand, which presents unique challenges for simulating user traffic and measuring performance.

Load testing tools need to integrate with serverless platforms (e.g., AWS Lambda, Azure Functions) to assess how serverless functions perform under load. This integration allows teams to evaluate the performance of serverless applications in a way that mirrors real-world usage.

End-to-End Testing:

In microservices and serverless environments, conducting end-to-end load tests that encompass multiple services is essential. This approach ensures that the entire system operates cohesively under load, identifying potential bottlenecks in the interactions between services.

JMeter and Locust can be configured to perform end-to-end load tests, simulating user workflows that span multiple services and measuring overall system performance.

The Importance of Security Testing in Load Testing

Integrating Security and Load Testing:

As organizations become increasingly aware of security threats, integrating security testing into load testing processes is essential. Performance tests can reveal vulnerabilities that may be exploited under high load conditions.

Load testing tools should incorporate security testing capabilities, allowing teams to identify potential security weaknesses while assessing application performance.

Conducting Security Load Tests:

Security load testing involves simulating attacks or attempts to breach the application's defenses while evaluating performance under load. This approach helps identify how the application behaves when subjected to both legitimate user traffic and malicious attempts.

Tools like JMeter can be extended with security testing plugins to incorporate security checks during load tests, ensuring that performance assessments are comprehensive.

Focus on Compliance:

With the increasing focus on regulatory compliance (e.g., GDPR, HIPAA), organizations must ensure that their applications meet both performance and security standards. Load testing can help validate that applications comply with security regulations while maintaining optimal performance.

Performance testing teams should work closely with security teams to align load testing strategies with security requirements, ensuring that all aspects of application performance are thoroughly evaluated.

The future of load testing with JMeter and Locust is poised to be shaped by emerging trends such as cloud-based testing, the integration of AI and machine learning, continuous performance testing practices, the rise of microservices and serverless architectures, and the growing importance of security in performance assessments. By embracing these trends, organizations can enhance their load testing strategies, ensuring that applications can handle the complexities of modern software development and deliver exceptional user experiences. As technology continues to evolve, staying ahead of these trends will empower teams to optimize performance testing efforts and maintain the highest standards of application performance.